Devils and Deviants

Devils and Deviants

Religious Schism in 1 and 2 John

Jason L. Merritt

☙PICKWICK *Publications* · Eugene, Oregon

DEVILS AND DEVIANTS
Religious Schism in 1 and 2 John

Copyright © 2017 Jason L. Merritt. All rights reserved. Except for brief quotations in critical publications or reviews, no part of this book may be reproduced in any manner without prior written permission from the publisher. Write: Permissions, Wipf and Stock Publishers, 199 W. 8th Ave., Suite 3, Eugene, OR 97401.

Pickwick Publications
An Imprint of Wipf and Stock Publishers
199 W. 8th Ave., Suite 3
Eugene, OR 97401

www.wipfandstock.com

PAPERBACK ISBN: 978-1-62032-917-7
HARDCOVER ISBN: 978-1-4982-8726-5
EBOOK ISBN: 978-1-5326-0562-8

Cataloguing-in-Publication data:

Names: Merritt, Jason L.

Title: Devils and deviants : religious schism in 1 and 2 John / Jason L. Merritt

Description: Eugene, OR: Pickwick Publications, 2017 | Includes bibliographical references.

Identifiers: ISBN 978-1-62032-917-7 (paperback) | ISBN 978-1-4982-8726-5 (hardcover) | ISBN 978-1-5326-0562-8 (ebook)

Subjects: LCSH: Bible. Epistle of John, 1st—Criticism, interpretation, etc. | Bible. Epistle of John, 2nd—Criticism, interpretation, etc.

Classification: LCC BS2805.3 M57 2017 (print) | LCC BS2805.3 (ebook)

Manufactured in the U.S.A.   01/23/17

To Christy, with all my love.
Your encouragement and support made this possible.

Contents

Acknowledgments | ix
Abbreviations | x

I   Introduction: Stating the Problem | 1

II   Modeling Religious Schism | 7
    Introduction | 7
    Preliminary Considerations | 8
    Motivation for Schism | 12
    Propensity to Schism | 20
    The Polemics of Schism | 36
    Exit Group Formation, the Discourse of Departure, and Defection | 47
    Retrospection | 56
    Schism Begets Schism | 58

III   Presuppositions Moving Forward | 62
    The Epistles and the Gospel | 62
    Schism in the Gospel? | 64
    The Johannine Literature and the Book of Revelation | 72
    The Question of 3 John | 74

Contents

IV Applying the Model | 76
    Rhetorical Analysis | 76
    Use of the Gospel and Revelation | 81
    The Johannine Community as Uniquely Legitimate | 82
    A Heterogeneous Group? | 101
    Arguing for Legitimacy | 112
    The Victimized Community | 124

V Conclusion | 135
    Previous Evaluations of the Problem | 135
    Constructing a Model | 136
    The Nature of the Community | 137
    Rhetorical Aim within the Setting of Religious Schism | 139

Bibliography | 141

Acknowledgments

THIS WORK WOULD NOT have been possible without my wife, who worked tirelessly to support our family while I worked my way through graduate school. Without her love and support, the process would have been extraordinarily more difficult, if even possible. My daughters, Mallorie, Kirah, and Annaliese, gave up a good deal of time with me as I researched and wrote, but are now very excited to know their dad will be a published author. I love you all.

Dr. Francisco Lozada had hardly finished moving into his office at Brite Divinity School before I asked him to direct my dissertation, and he bravely agreed. His feedback and guidance during the writing process were invaluable to me and I am eternally grateful to him for his graciousness and friendship. Prior to Dr. Lozada's arrival, Dr. Carolyn Osiek gave me invaluable feedback—as well as wise counsel—as I began developing and applying the model that would become my dissertation. Prior to his departure to Pacific Lutheran Theological Seminary, Dr. David Balch was a rich source of information, kindness, and direction. Thanks to Dr. Leo Perdue, as well, for his helpful feedback. Finally, a special thanks to my friend and colleague, Dr. Wade Berry, for allowing me on many occasions to disrupt his schedule so that I could talk through the knotty issues that arise during writing.

Abbreviations

AB	Anchor Bible
ABR	*Australian Biblical Review*
ABRL	Anchor Bible Reference Library
ANTC	Abingdon New Testament Commentaries
ASR	*American Sociological Review*
BBET	Beiträge zur biblischen Exegese und Theologie
BECNT	Baker Exegetical Commentary on the New Testament
BNTC	Black's New Testament Commentaries
BRS	The Biblical Resource Series
BZAW	Beihefte zur Zeitschrift für die alttestamentliche Wissenschaft
CBQ	*Catholic Biblical Quarterly*
CC	Continental Commentary
ExpTim	*Expository Times*
FF	Foundations & Facets: Social Facets
GBS	Guides to Biblical Scholarship
HNTC	Harper's New Testament Commentaries
ICC	International Critical Commentary
IBC	Interpretation
JSNT	*Journal for the Study of the New Testament*
JSSR	*Journal for the Scientific Study of Religion*
JTS	*Journal of Theological Studies*
KEK	Kritisch-exegetischer Kommentar

Abbreviations

LCL	Loeb Classical Library
NAC	New American Commentary
NCB	New Century Bible Commentary
NCBC	New Cambridge Bible Commentary
NG	*National Geographic*
NIB	New Interpreter's Bible
NIBC	New International Biblical Commentary
NICNT	New International Commentary on the New Testament
NIGTC	New International Greek Testament Commentary
NTL	New Testamnet Library
NTS	*New Testament Studies*
NovTSup	Supplements to *Novum Testamentum*
OTL	Old Testament Library
OTKNT	Ökumenischer Taschenbuchkommentar zum Neuen Testament
PNTC	Pillar New Testament Commentary
RBS	Resources for Biblical Study
SP	Sacra Pagina
SPNT	Studies on Personalities of the New Testament
THKNT	Theologischer Handkommentar zum Neuen Testament
TNTC	Tyndale New Testament Commentaries
TSAJ	Texts and Studies in Ancient Judaism
TTS	Texts and Translations Series
TU	*Texte und Unterschungen*
VCSup	Supplements to Viligiae Christianae
WBC	Word Biblical Commentary
WTJ	*Westminster Theological Journal*
WUNT	Wissenschaftliche Untersuchungen zum Neuen Testament
YPR	Yale Publications in Religion
ZTK	*Zeitschrift für Theologie und Kirche*

I

Introduction: Stating the Problem

"They went out of us, but they were not of us." 1 John 2:19a

"... many false prophets have gone out into the world." 1 John 4:1b[1]

THAT A SCHISM OCCURRED within the Johannine community prior to the writing of 1 and 2 John is virtually universally accepted within modern Johannine studies.[2] However, within that universal agreement regarding the fact of the schism, there exists a considerable degree of diversity of opinion regarding the role of the schism in prompting the writing of 1 and 2 John, as well as the nature of the schismatics' beliefs and our ability to discern it.

---

1. Both passages are my translation.

2. Two items ought to be unpacked here, only one page into this study. The definition of "Johannine community" is one of some debate within contemporary Johannine studies. A full rehearsal of the debate is neither necessary nor prudent for this study; a simple statement of my position within the discussion should suffice: by "Johannine community," I mean a network of churches, most likely located in western Asia Minor, with their primary place of activity centered on Ephesus, whose understanding of the person and work of Jesus of Nazareth are best represented in the Gospel of John. From this community emerged three epistles—1, 2, and 3 John—and possibly Revelation (a highly disputed point, which I will discuss much later). The second issue at hand is the inclusion of 1 and 2 John in this study and the exclusion of 3 John. Third John is generally seen as reflective of events and developments within the Johannine community that are unrelated to the schism. While I believe that 3 John can be understood within the context of the schism, that understanding is admittedly ambiguous. The inclusion of 3 John in the present study would raise more questions than it would answer. With those considerations in mind, I leave the discussion of 3 John and its potential relationship to the schism for a later study.

Devils and Deviants

From the mid-nineteenth century until the turn of the current century, scholarly inquiry into the Johannine Epistles produced a variety of methodological approaches to these brief texts, and, not surprisingly, a variety of results. Popular at the time, but largely abandoned now, is Rudolph Bultmann's redaction-critical approach to the Epistles.[3] B. F. Westcott's earlier methodological approach to the Epistles has had more staying power than Bultmann's, but his narrow identification of the schismatics with the historical figure of Cerinthus has been determined too specific by later scholarship.[4] Raymond Brown's more recent attempt to understand the positions of both the epistolary author and the schismatics as somehow drawn from the theology of the Gospel of John represents something of a corrective to Westcott and has continued to have some degree of acceptance in current scholarship.[5] A brief overview, but sufficient to illustrate the diversity of approaches taken to the question and the answer yielded.

This diversity, while fruitful for dialogue, has led to a growing sense that the task of recovering the beliefs of the schismatics is, ultimately, impossible. The task of recovery depends upon the accuracy and thoroughness with which the epistolary author reports about the beliefs of the schismatics, and neither can be guaranteed. Indeed, it is now common to point out the fact that there may be as few as two clear references to the schismatics in 1 John and that neither reference really tells us anything of their beliefs, and may even be construed as referring to two distinct groups. What then is modern scholarship to do with 1 and 2 John if, as scholarship had asserted for nearly 150 years, they are polemical texts to be understood within the framework of a religious schism and that they are best understood when they can be read against the (unrecoverable) beliefs of the schismatics?

Increasingly, that question has been answered with a reformulation of the entire approach to interpreting the epistles: rather than understand 1 and 2 John as polemical texts that are written as a response to the recent schism, might it be more profitable to read them as somehow being non-polemical, with the recent schism being more of a minor incident that is actually receiving only passing mention rather than being the primary motivation for the composition of the Epistles?

---

3. See Bultmann, *The Johannine Epistles*.

4. Westcott, *The Epistles of St. John*, xxxiv.

5. Brown, *The Epistles of John*. Bultmann's redactional approach and Brown's use of John's Gospel to understand the theology of both the epistolary author and the schismatics continue to resonate in contemporary scholarship. See in particular Wahlde, *The Gospel and Letters of John*.

Introduction: Stating the Problem

Judith Lieu was the first to offer a sustained critique of the pursuit of the identity and beliefs of the opponents in 1 John. Her primary critique is of the overuse of second-century parallels in attempting to discern the beliefs of the schismatics. Instead of reading 1 John as a polemical text and attempting to reconstruct the beliefs of the opponents from it, Lieu argues that the epistolary author writes to assure his readers (and, it would seem, himself) that they do indeed possess eternal life.[6] Lieu allows that the schism had occurred and that it had prompted the composition of 1 John, but the purpose of its composition was not to attack the opponents but to examine the beliefs and ethics of the Johannine community with the goal of said reassurance.[7] As such, 1 John is loosely connected to the schism in that the departure of the opponents prompted the introspection that leads to the composition of the letter. Lieu leaves undefined the need for reassurance. Has the schism shaken the confidence of the members of the Johannine community? Do they now doubt that they chose the correct side in the debate that preceded the schism? These questions are left unasked, and, therefore, unanswered.

Schmid carries the conversation forward by developing a theory of reading based on intertextuality and systems theory that limits or completely removes the need for historical reconstructions.[8] Based on intertextuality, Schmid argues that both the Gospel of John and 1 John can be read in reference to one another and that this mutual referentiality is independent of chronology, i.e. that one does not need to know which was composed first in order to read them effectively in light of one another. By this means, Schmid is able to read the Gospel and the 1 John together as a self-referential literary system in which historical events and persons are disconnected from their environments and become a literary device by which the author speaks about himself. In this way, Schmid can speak of the opponents as being "creations" of the epistolary author.[9] Again, in this scenario, the point of the Epistle is to reassure the reader: " . . . the opponent texts operate as a basis for the ethical parenesis: having surpassed the scenario of danger, the reader returns strengthened to the ethical issues. Moreover, the main function of the two texts is not to deal with the opponents and their

---

6. Lieu, "Authority to Become Children of God," 210–28. Lieu repeats the critique in her commentary on 1 and 2 John, and in her subsequent commentary on 1–3 John.

7. Ibid., 225.

8. Schmid, "How to Read the First Epistle of John Non-polemically," 24–41.

9. Ibid., 33.

position, but to articulate words of encouragement to the reader so that the opponents are rather an instrument of self-assurance." [10] Schmid's model for reading is fascinating, and not without its merits, but we here find him including the very kinds of reconstructed historical events that his model claims are unnecessary, and we are still left wondering why the Johannine Christians find themselves in need of reassurance.

Daniel Streett's recent study in a non-polemical reading contains a virtual catalogue of the various proposals that have been made regarding the identity of the schismatics, as well as thorough explications of the problems inherent in each proposal.[11] Indeed, the wide variety of reconstructions ought to caution us against the endeavor. The epistolary author gives us precious little that we might use in reconstructing the beliefs of the schismatics, and what little that is given comes to us through the lens of the epistolary author's own theology and his negative experience with the schismatics. He is not an objective reporter of facts, and we should not pretend that he is. However, if such a reconstruction is untenable, how ought we to read the Epistles? Street represents something of a synthesis of recent non-polemical readings when he advocates for a "pastoral" motivation for the writing of the 1 John which has as its purpose pastoral caution and reassurance grounded in ethical teaching.[12]

Those who advocate for a non-polemical reading have rightly pointed out the deficiencies of readings which attempt to reconstruct the beliefs of the opponents.[13] However, their own proposals raise new questions for which there are no ready answers. Further, while not disputing that a schism has taken place in the Johannine community, they very consciously avoid positing a significant connection between the issues involved in the schism and the writing of the Epistles. Should we deny that this schism had little if any impact on the writing of these epistles simply because we cannot reconstruct the beliefs of such opponents? That would seem to be a case of throwing the baby out with the bathwater, and it is really the crux of the attempt to read the epistles "non-polemically."

---

10. Ibid., 36.

11. Streett, *They Went out from Us*, 8–111.

12. Ibid., 118–31.

13. The non-polemical reading is not limited to the authors discussed here. See also Griffith, *Keep Yourselves from Idols*; Griffith, "A Non-polemical Reading of 1 John," 253–76; and Jobes, *1, 2, & 3 John*, 24.

Introduction: Stating the Problem

It is telling that in this nascent dialogue regarding the polemical or non-polemical nature of the Epistles that we have not defined either term. Implicit in the discussion is the question of whether or not the epistolary author is addressing—whether directly or indirectly—the opponents, the schismatics. The advocates for a non-polemical reading correctly note that the schismatics are not part of the intended audience. Rather, the epistolary author is addressing the members of his community, and this question of audience is a contributing factor in understanding the Epistles as non-polemical. In other words, there seems to be an implicit understanding of "polemic" as being directed toward a specific audience. If the epistolary author is in some way addressing the schismatics, then the Epistles are polemical. If the epistolary author is speaking to his own followers in order to reassure them, then they are pastoral rather than polemical. Might it be better to understand a text as polemical based on its tone and rhetorical function? Might the pastoral goal of assurance be accomplished through a polemical attack on the schismatics? That, to me, seems a reasonable alternative to the either/or construct of recent scholarly debate.

While the non-polemical reading of 1 and 2 John serves as a necessary caution against too confident a reconstruction of the beliefs of the schismatics, I am not convinced that the schism plays at best a minor role in the composition of the Epistles, and continue to believe that they can be understood as polemical texts, even if the schismatics are not part of the intended audience. Indeed, the anthropological and sociological study of schism has been little used in understanding early Christian documents and history, but presents us with the opportunity for rich study of the processes by which early Christianity separated itself from Judaism, and the processes by which smaller groups within the larger Christian group or groups separated themselves from one another.[14]

The primary point to make in this introduction is that schism tends to be a traumatic event in the life of a community, and the trauma tends to be more profound when the parent group (the group from which the

14. The anthropological and sociological study of schism primarily centers upon religious schism, but also includes a significant amount of work done in the realm of political schism. It is important to note at the outset that the experts in this field do not see religious schism and political schism as discrete events. Rather, they view the process of schism as something of a universal pattern of human behavior that functions the same regardless of its precise context, be it religious or political. There is much interplay between those who study religious schism and those who study religious schism, and the present study will make use of studies in political schism along with studies in religious schism.

schismatics separate themselves) itself is also small. The trauma of the schism tends to be alleviated through the repeated discussion of the events, and this process of "talking through" the trauma can actually take some time. In some cases, the bitterness of the schism can still be detected within one or both groups decades or even centuries after the actual schism. For this reason, we ought to be cautious when we accept the fact of the schism but deny its impact on the composition of the Epistles.

Better than rejecting the impact of the schism on the Epistles, we might read the Epistles as part of the process of "talking through" the trauma of the recent schism. Indeed, as we shall see, it is quite possible to read the Epistles as an attempt on the part of the epistolary author to persuade the "fence riders" that they have made the right decision in remaining within his community, and it is his intention to solidify that decision by contrasting his fidelity to the tradition, access to the tradition's legitimating institutions, and ethical behavior with the "progressive" theology and unethical behavior of the schismatics. In that regard, the Epistles are not addressed to the schismatics but can certainly be understood as exhibiting a polemical tone. Further, such a proposal has the advantage of acknowledging the author's goal of pastoral assurance as argued by the non-polemicists, while closely connecting the need for that assurance with the recent schism.

But this study is not meant to be a mere defense of the polemical reading of 1 and 2 John. The formal study of schism allows us to construct an overarching framework, an heuristic lens, that allows us to examine the Epistles for additional evidence of the schism that might otherwise evade our notice. By pulling together studies of schisms from across history and cultures, we can construct a comprehensive model of schism that allows us to see the institutional and structural causes of schism, the pattern by which cliques begin to talk themselves out of the parent group, the back-and-forth process by which the clique and parent group attempt to appropriate legitimating institutions, and the aftermath of schism for both the parent group and the clique. As we will see, there are elements of 1 and 2 John not typically connected to the schism that can be understood quite well within this overarching framework. The picture that emerges is one that is thoroughly compatible with the model and that may actually give us some insight into the history and composition of the Johannine community, even if the nature of the schismatics' theology still remains beyond recovery. We will now turn to the construction of that model.

II

Modeling Religious Schism

Introduction

THAT A SCHISM WITHIN the Johannine community is reflected in at least 1 and 2 John is not under any serious doubt, and the cause of that schism has attracted a great deal of attention from scholarship. That attention, however, has primarily been directed at the schismatics and their beliefs. The difficulty with this focus is that anything we might know of the schismatics is mediated to us through the epistolary author, and his perspective is not one of an unbiased reporter of objective facts. Indeed, he is intimately concerned with achieving certain goals by writing his epistles and casts the schismatics in such a light as to best accomplish those goals. It is not his intent to report to his recipients the entire theological framework of the schismatics—indeed, his recipients are likely quite familiar with that framework. Rather, he highlights those elements with which he disagrees most strongly, and does so with the intent of convincing his readers that the schismatics are wrong to hold such views and that they themselves have made the correct choice by remaining faithful to the teachings of the community as represented by the epistolary author.

And yet, the process of one group separating itself from another is not unique to the Johannine community. Indeed, it is and has been carried out in both religious and non-religious groups in a variety of social and historical contexts, and anthropological and sociological work in this area reveal to us that the process is carried out with a remarkable degree of consistency and predictability. From this work, we can construct a relatively comprehensive model of the process of schism which we can then apply to 1 and 2 John in an effort to sift through the author's rhetoric in order to isolate the evidence of the structural and ideological factors that contributed to the schism, the process by which the schism was effected, and the after-effects of the schism on the Johannine community.

Preliminary Considerations

Any discussion of schism within the Johannine community as reflected in the Epistles ought to begin with at least a cursory examination of the scholarly discussion of schism within the Johannine community as reflected in the Gospel, and that discussion ought to begin with the work of J. Louis Martyn. Since Martyn published the first edition of *History and Theology in the Fourth Gospel*, it has become an axiom in Johannine studies that the Johannine community suffered a forcible expulsion from the synagogue prior to the composition of the Gospel.[1] In other words, the Johannine community experienced a religious schism. Martyn's work was historical and literary in approach and has spawned several subsequent and divergent studies on the Johannine community and its history, and social scientific criticism has not avoided this topic. However, those who have approached this question from a social scientific perspective have generally done so by examining the Gospel with an anti-society and anti-language model.

The first of these studies was W. Meeks' "The Man from Heaven in Johannine Sectarianism."[2] Through his analysis, Meeks argues that, "Only a reader who is thoroughly familiar with the whole Fourth Gospel or else acquainted by some non-literary means with its symbolism and developing themes . . . can possibly understand its double entendre and its abrupt transitions. For the outsider—even for an interested inquirer (like Nicodemus)—the dialogue is opaque."[3] His examination leads him to the conclusion that, "as long as we approach the Johannine literature as a chapter in the history of *ideas*, it will defy our understanding . . . .But if we pose our questions in the form, What functions did this particular system of metaphors have for the group that developed it? then even its self-contradictions and its disjunctures may be seen to be *means of communication*."[4]

---

1. The following discussion will bear out how standard this view has become.

2. Meeks, "The Man from Heaven in Johannine Sectarianism," 44–72.

3. Ibid., 57. Another implication of Meeks's discussion is that the point of this opaque language is to reaffirm to the informed reader that Jesus is superior to John the Baptist and Nicodemus, as are his followers by association.

4. Ibid., 68.

Malina and Rohrbaugh have adopted Meeks' view of the language of John's Gospel as intentionally opaque and use a model of anti-societies and anti-language to understand John's Gospel.[5] More recently, David Reed[6] has used a similar model to argue that the separation of the Johannine community from the synagogue occurred because the community, an anti-society, chose to make its private transcript public, a transcript in which Jesus is depicted as being superior to the emperor. This publication drew the ire of the synagogue leaders, who feared Roman retribution for such claims by a group embedded within the synagogue, thus leading to the separation.[7]

Social-scientific criticism's interest in schism within the Johannine community has centered on the Gospel and the separation of the Johannine community from Judaism, and its more specific methodological model has been that of anti-society and anti-language. The present study attempts to correct this rather one-sided approach by focusing on the Epistles rather than the Gospel, and by using a model of religious schism rather than one of anti-society and anti-language. It ought to be noted that the sociological and anthropological study of religious schism is a field that is not fully developed even within the fields of sociology and anthropology, a fact that is often noted by sociologists and anthropologists. Liebman, Sutton, and Wuthnow lamented:

> Issues of denominationalism and sectarianism have long fascinated sociologists . . . but they have paid little attention to schisms. While schisms have been recognized as a major source of new religious denominations, empirical research on the determinants of schisms remains sparse . . . Given the theoretical and practical significance of religious schisms, we anticipated finding

---

5. Malina and Rohrbaugh, *A Social Science Commentary on the Gospel of John*, 4–15. Malina and Rohrbaugh also adopt Martyn's thesis in its essentials, i.e., that expulsion is anachronism and the expulsion is probably associated with the *birkath ha-minim*.

6 Reed, "Rethinking John's Social Setting," 93–106.

7. Incidentally, the assertions of Meeks, Malina and Rohrbaugh, and Reed have not gone unnoticed or unchallenged by other interpreters of the Johannine literature. Culpepper, *Anatomy of the Fourth Gospel*, 187, describes as "exaggerated" Meeks's evaluation of Johannine language as obscure. Koester, *Symbolism in the Fourth* 18–24, directly argues against Malina and Rohrbaugh in asserting that John's Gospel assumes a mixed readership of those who are highly informed and those who are not. While this argument is not without its difficulties (the evidence he cites can be attributed to multiple sources, redaction, and the development of the community from a Jewish synagogue-sect to a missionary community that included Gentiles), there is still an element of plausibility in his argument.

a large body of published literature on the subject. However . . . our own exploration of the major journals, books, denominational histories, and unpublished papers netted only a few studies.[8]

Zuckerman, writing over a decade later, confirms their earlier findings by simply saying, "Indeed, there is little out there."[9] For this reason, the model that I propose will, of necessity, draw upon a number of different researchers who have written on various aspects of this process, rather than relying on a comprehensive model constructed by a single researcher or group of researchers, since no such comprehensive model yet exists. Additionally, I will make use of examinations of schism within both religious and political contexts. While individual researchers tend to be more interested in one over the other, there is general agreement within the field that the process of schism plays out the same in both contexts.

The process of schism necessarily involves at least two participating groups: (1) the schismatic group which removes itself from or is removed by (2) the parent group.[10] For this reason, any complete model of religious schism that I might hope to construct must take into account the parts played by both groups even if the primary concern of this study is for the self-understanding of the parent group, the Johannine church(es). Therefore, for the sake of fully disclosing the model from which I will be operating, I will fully articulate the roles of both groups in the schismatic process even though I will give far more attention to the epistolary author's viewpoint in applying the model to the text of 1 and 2 John. What follows, then, is a general outline and description of the "component parts" of a religious schism and, when taken as a whole, constitutes my model.

Before proceeding, however, an additional note is in order. Social-scientific criticism has critically evaluated classical historical-critical methodology for its failure to make explicit its presuppositions and interpretive models, and so has strongly emphasized the need for detailed and

---

8. Liebman, Sutton, and Wuthnow, "Exploring the Social Sources of Denominationalism," 343–52; quoted in Zuckerman, *Strife*, 91.

9. Zuckerman, *Strife*, 91.

10. There is a certain degree of diversity in the terminology used by the various researchers upon whom we will draw in this chapter. Further, the terminology employed must, of necessity, be flexible so that we may more accurately describe each phase of the schism. For that reason, there will be some variation in the terminology we employ here in describing the two opposing groups in the schismatic dance. The parent group will at different times also be referred to as the larger movement and the larger group. The schismatic group will also be referred to as clique, faction, and exit group.

clearly articulated interpretive models presented prior to interpretation.[11] In addition, a fundamental, if not *the* fundamental, presupposition of social-scientific criticism is that there is a great deal of difference between the first-century Mediterranean people who produced the Bible and post-Enlightenment, northern European people who have produced much of biblical scholarship currently in use. The interpreter, so the social-scientific critic cautions, must be aware of this difference lest she or he read the biblical texts anachronistically. However, there is often a disjuncture between the models proposed and the emphasis upon the differences between readers modern and ancient: models for understanding these ancient texts are very often drawn from modern, Western contexts without attempting to demonstrate from the outset that the modern research is directly applicable to the ancient social situation despite the proposed cultural differences. Esler, for instance, is at pains to highlight the anachronistic way in which Romans is often read by modern scholarship and emphasizes the need for a reading rooted in not only the historical but also the social situation of the letter. However, he then proceeds to offer as his model for reading Romans the work of Tajfel, who studied social identity and intergroup phenomena among American boys in summer camps in the 1950s.[12] Similarly, Malina and Rohrbaugh begin their commentary on John by emphasizing the differences between modern and ancient social contexts, but proceed to construct a model of anti-society and anti-language illustrated primarily through the U.S. drug culture.[13]

To put it plainly, social scientific criticism argues for particularity, but practices a kind of universality. This criticism is not offered in order to argue that the models drawn from modern cultures cannot be applied to ancient situations, thereby undermining the work of these scholars. It is simply meant to point out a rather glaring oversight. The present study acknowledges that first-century Mediterranean people viewed the world and interacted with one another in ways different than those of the various types of modern readers. However, I will also note that, while there are degrees of diversity within this schismatic process, the process itself tends to work itself out in a remarkably consistent way across time and cultures. For this

---

11. Elliott, *What is Social-Scientific Criticism?* 36, 40–41.

12. Esler, *Conflict and Identity in Romans*, 3–8, 19–39. An immediate problem that one might see with this proposal is that the basically individualistic orientation of modern Americans clashes with the basically dyadic orientation of ancient Mediterraneans. Cf. Bruce J. Malina, *The New Testament World*, 58–76.

13. Malina and Rohrbaugh, *Social-Science Commentary on the Gospel of John*, 2–20.

reason, I will intentionally construct my model from a variety of schismatic studies that focus on schism within different cultures in different time periods. My hope is that the model itself will demonstrate that it is applicable to the social milieu in which 1 and 2 John were written. I would also finally note that the process of schism can be complex in the sense that certain aspects of the process tend to overlap one another, and other aspects of the scientific study of schism tend to run like a thread throughout the whole of the process. While always remaining aware of these complexities, I will endeavor to present the model as clearly and as simply as possible, though some readers will surely disagree with certain aspects of my organization and categorization.

Motivations for Schism

Basic to the study of schism is the question of the motivation for schism. What drives one group to separate itself from another? One can see in the scholarly literature movement away from a narrow, materialistic view of motivation for schism toward a more broad view.

Seminal to the sociological study of the motivation for schism is H. Richard Niebuhr's work in *The Social Sources of Denominationalism*. As one might infer from the title, Niebuhr's position is that religious schism does not occur "simply" for theological or ideological reasons;[14] rather, social forces produce division. Niebuhr summarizes his position:

> One phase of denominationalism is largely explicable by means of a modified economic interpretation of religious history; for the divisions of the church have been occasioned more frequently by the direct and indirect operation of economic factors than by the influence of any other major interest of man [sic]. Furthermore, it is evident that economic stratification is often responsible for maintaining divisions which were originally due to differences of another sort.[15]

Niebuhr further argues that the economic disparities that give rise to schism (or, in his terminology, denominationalism)[16] often have their ori-

---

14. The term "ideological" is preferred over "theological" in schismatic studies given that the field embraces the study of schism in both religious and non-religious settings.

15. Niebuhr, *Social Sources of Denominationalism*, 26.

16. Niebuhr was not only interested in what caused schisms within denominations, but also focused on why certain denominations continued to attract and retain certain

gins in racial divisions which become entrenched economic divisions and can be seen in the tensions between native inhabitants and immigrants, nationalism, and cultural and ethnic differences. The end result is that such heterogeneous groups will almost inevitably tend toward schism given the number of competing interests represented within the group. Thus schism is a sociological rather than theological or ideological phenomenon.

Niebuhr's proposal attained and maintained an axiomatic position within schismatic studies for a number of decades, and subsequent research into the topic seemed to confirm his observations. Two early studies focused more specifically on schism, rather than Niebuhr's more general concern with denominationalism. Dawson, in what may be described as a more philosophical or theological than sociological article, argues that the source of schism in Christianity lay primarily in nationalism and nationalist culture. Referring to such varied schismatic episodes in Christian history as the schism between the Byzantine and Armenian churches on the one hand and the Protestant Reformation on the other, Dawson repeatedly points out socio-political issues that gave rise to a sense of alienation among the effected peoples. A religious or theological issue was championed as a means of opposing their political enemies, thus leading to schism. In this way, Dawson is able to assert:

> Thus we are brought up once more against the fundamental problem of Christian disunity which is the problem of schism. In practice this problem is so closely associated with that of heresy, i.e. difference of religious belief, that they are apt to be confused with one another. But it is nevertheless important to distinguish them carefully, and to consider the nature of schism in itself, for I believe that it is in the question of schism rather than that of heresy that the key to the problem of the disunity of Christendom is to be found. For heresy as a rule is not the cause of schism but an excuse for it, or rather a rationalization of it. Behind every heresy lies some kind of social conflict, and it is only by the resolution of this conflict that unity can be restored.[17]

Tubeville's study was also an early confirmation of Niebuhr's conclusions, though he draws more directly upon the work of Dawson, given that

---

classes of people. He was followed in this interest by Pope, *Millhands and Preachers*, who examined the social make up of the congregations of Gaston County, North Carolina, and confirmed Niebuhr's findings by concluding that the various congregations could be easily divided along class lines.

17. Dawson, "What about Heretics," 514.

Dawson specifically examined religious schism rather than denominationalism generally. Tubeville's study, however, was more a straightforward sociological study than was Dawson's and so merits a more detailed treatment here. His study examines a schism that occurred within a local Methodist congregation in Turbeville, South Carolina but which had significance for the newly reunited Methodist church nationally. The schism was immediately precipitated by the unification of the three main Methodist traditions in the United States: the Methodist Protestant Church; the Methodist Episcopal Church; and the Methodist Episcopal Church, South. The Pine Grove congregation in Turbeville, which had belonged to the Methodist Episcopal Church, South, eventually split over the issue of unification, initially meeting as separate congregations at different times within the same church building, but eventually becoming embroiled in a protracted legal battle. Turbeville's study, however, demonstrates that the roots of the schism preceded the controversial unification of the three branches of Methodism and were social rather than theological.

The beginnings of schism can be traced to the onset of the Great Depression and the social and economic upheaval that it caused. Two specific aspects of the Depression set Pine Grove on the path toward religious schism: (1) scarcity of and the need to procure material goods, and (2) residential instability. The economic pressures of the Depression created a situation in which members of the community had limited access to material goods and conveniences. One family, the Summervilles,[18] took the lead in obtaining these goods and conveniences for the community and were "instrumental in getting a church, school, and post office for the community."[19] The instability of the population, however, led to a number of families leaving to seek a better economic situation elsewhere. Subsequently, people from outside the community arrived and took up residence in Turbeville. Among these families were the Browns, Newberrys, and Bettors.[20] The newcomers resented the prominent place of the Summervilles within the community, reasoning that "they had representatives fully as capable as the Summervilles, and saw no reason why they should not be community leaders."[21] A schismatic dance[22] ensued with the two parties

---

18. Tubeville provides pseudonyms for all the participants.
19. Ibid., 32.
20. Again, the names are pseudonyms.
21. Tubeville, "Religious Schism," 32.
22. "Schismatic dance" is a term used to describe the oppositional dynamic that

taking opposite sides on an increasing number of issues, up to and including the unification of the three Methodist churches in 1939. By this time the Pine Grove congregation had aligned itself into two parties: that led by the Summervilles and that led by the Browns, Newberrys, and Bettors. The latter group, Tubeville notes, was financially better off than the former.[23] When the question of the congregation's support of unification arose, the faction led by the Summervilles supported the proposal; predictably, the other faction opposed it, leading to the split of the congregation and subsequent legal action.

Tubeville's conclusion, then, is that the schism that occurred in the community and whose purported cause was an ecclesiastical/theological issue could actually be attributed to social and economic factors that had arisen long before this particular ecclesiastical/theological issue came into play, thus supporting Niebuhr's perspective. Indeed, the ecclesiastical/theological issue seems to have served only as a good excuse for enacting a separation that had long been desired for wholly other reasons.

In the 1950s and early 1960s, interest in the part played in schism by ambition and/or personal antipathy began to rise, and a number of productive studies were conducted in this area. S. L. Greenslade was the first to propose this connection, though hesitatingly: "The personal factor is always important, but rarely, if ever, the sole cause of schism. Occasionally, though not, as it happened, in the most widespreading and most enduring schisms, it was the main cause . . . ."[24] Wilson also advocates for this possibility, arguing that, "Schism in Christian Science has almost invariably been among the teachers of the movement, and has almost always been centred on the struggle for power" and that, "Clashes of personality, perhaps specifically concerned with ambition to lead, appear to have been at the basis of most schism in Christadelphianism."[25] Greenslade expands this idea, arguing that ambitions and the clashes thereof may be located not

---

develops during the process of the separation of the schismatic group from the parent group. The two parties metaphorically stand face-to-face and react to the movements of the other. For an example of its use in a study of schism, see Zuckerman, *Strife*, 238.

23. Tubeville, "Religious Schism," 33.

24. Greenslade, *Schism*. Greenslade's work does not seek to construct a single motivation for schism, but proposes several, including the traditional socioeconomic motivation. He was, however, somewhat ahead of his time by arguing that, in some cases, ideological disputes should be taken at face value. Cf. ibid., 90–124, where he discusses liturgical disputes and puritanism in this light.

25. Wilson, *Sects and Society*, 340–41.

in opposed individuals, but groups.²⁶ Calley, in his study of West Indian Pentecostal sects in England, accepts the theory of ambition as a source of schism, but qualifies it:

> Although some leaders of breakaway movements may cold-bloodedly invent a doctrinal dispute after having decided to start a Church of their own, I doubt whether this is very often the case. The situation is rather that personal ambition and general dissatisfaction go hand-in-hand with a searching of the scripture for an explanation for the dissatisfaction. The saint tries to discover in biblical terms why he (*sic*) feels restless and dissatisfied.²⁷

Calley's focus here on dissatisfaction offers a foreshadowing of the work of Doherty, who argues that the roots of schism within sectarian movements can be found in a sense of alienation from the world.

Doherty's study of the Hicksite/Orthodox schism within the Society of Friends in 1827 represents both a continuation and a broadening of the search for social reasons for schism.²⁸ Through careful historical research into the social location of the members of the Orthodox and Hicksite factions within the Society, Doherty argues that one's choice of the Orthodox or Hicksite faction would have been predetermined by one's social location, with the wealthy becoming Orthodox and the less wealthy becoming Hicksite.²⁹ His conclusion, then, is that the Hicksite split was "clearly conditioned by socioeconomic pressures."³⁰ But such summary statements actually obscure the complexity of his reconstruction of the schism, for the economic factors were not themselves the direct reasons for the composition of the two factions. Rather, economic conditions contributed to a *sense of alienation from the world or the lack of such a sense*; it is this perception of alienation that directly contributed to the make up of the two factions.³¹ Doherty works from a model of sectarianism that understands sects as drawing their strength from the alienation felt by its members.³² However,

---

26. Greenslade, *Schism*, 74–89. Specifically, Greenslade refers to sees and other ecclesiastical jurisdictions, citing the conflict between Rome and the eastern patriarchates as a prime example.

27. Calley, *God's People*, 51.

28. Doherty, *The Hicksite Separation*.

29. Ibid., 44.

30. Ibid., 50.

31. Ibid., 33–35.

32. Ibid., 34, defines alienation as a sense of tension and estrangement "that provokes

sects inevitably become imbalanced in their attempt to coordinate their relationships with "the world, religious organization and doctrine, and membership."[33] The response of the sect to this imbalance is, sooner or later, to move in "a churchly direction,"[34] which entails an increased acceptance of the world brought about by a lessening sense of alienation on the part of the elite leaders of the sect. The sect leaders then generally come under critique by those members of the sect who still have a high sense of alienation. Re-formation of the sect is then attempted by the elite, and, consequently, those sectarians whose sense of alienation is still high tend to separate from the group.[35] In the case of the Hicksite/Orthodox schism, the Orthodox faction was composed of wealthy, urban merchants who had succeeded in the business world, had become civic leaders, had developed friendships with those outside the Society, and felt the pressure of rising external criticism of the Society by evangelical Protestants. These Friends wanted to move the society in a more "churchly" direction by placing stress upon doctrine rather than the traditional behavioral emphasis of the Society.[36] The Hicksites, on the other hand, represented a less wealthy underclass that had suffered economically in recent years and so felt a higher sense of alienation from the world. Inevitably, schism did indeed occur at the 1829 annual Meeting, with the Hicksites withdrawing from the Society.[37] Doherty's work continues to place emphasis on social factors, but introduces a new note of complexity by taking into account the varying

---

a rejection of at least some significant portions of prevailing culture standards."

33. Ibid.

34. Ibid.

35. Ibid., 34–35.

36. As a point of clarification, "Orthodox" does not mean that this group championed Societal orthodoxy. Quite the contrary; they desired to move in the direction of orthodoxy as defined by their evangelical Protestant contemporaries. The Hicksites, for the most part, represented traditional Societal values.

37. Baer, *Recreating Utopia in the Desert*, 12–25, examines schism within the Church of Jesus Christ of Latter Day Saints and comes to remarkably similar conclusions as does Doherty, and seems to do so independently of Doherty's work. Baer broadly follows the development of LDS from a social protest movement that was largely alienated from the surrounding culture to a movement that became quite assimilated into the larger society. In the process, LDS became one of the most financially prosperous religious organizations in the world and repudiated polygamy in order to stave off criminal investigations. This financial success and repudiation of polygamy came with the price of the alienation of many of the members residing in the lower financial strata of the movement who also held to polygamous marriage as a means of securing the most paradisiacal afterlife possible. The result was a number of schisms, detailed on ibid., 25–46.

degrees of alienation felt by sectarians and the imbalance that this causes within the group. Passed over in Doherty's model, however, is a group for which he cannot account and which signaled a new direction in later schismatic studies: the "altruists."

In describing the different types of persons likely to become part of a sectarian group, Doherty labels as "altruists" those "who seem to seek no benefit for themselves but whose purposes are defined in terms of their own psychological needs."[38] This label remains rather nebulous until Doherty later begins to describe a subgroup within the Hicksite faction whose social location fit better with the Orthodox than with the Hicksites, with whom they sided. These tended to be of a more liberal theological persuasion and saw the Orthodox as stifling free inquiry and intolerant of diversity.[39] These, Doherty explains, are the altruists, the members of the schismatic faction who do not fit the profile of less wealthy and highly alienated. In other words, these are members who are motivated not by social factors, but by *ideology*.[40]

Doherty's undeveloped observation of the "altruists" within the Hicksite/Orthodox schism presages the work of Zuckerman, who has contributed significantly to schismatic studies by pointing out and developing two important motivations for schism: (1) ideology, and (2) personal relationship with the group leader.[41]

Zuckerman's study examines a schism that occurred in Temple Am Israel, a Conservative congregation in Willamette, Oregon in the early to mid-1990s. The schismatic dance began slowly in Temple Am Israel as certain ideological differences began to come to the fore in the congregation's communal life. The Rabbi, Moishe Kohner, began to take an active stance in support of Palestinian concerns in the Israeli-Palestinian conflict, going so far as to place a Palestinian flag alongside the Israeli flag in the sanctuary of the Temple. Gender issues also began to come into play as certain members of the congregation began to push for Reconstructionist practice

---

38. Doherty, *Hicksite Separation*, 11.

39. Ibid., 84.

40. This is not to say that ideology can be divorced from social factors, that ideology can be formed in a vacuum. Certainly there must be social factors that have shaped the ideology of the altruists, but they cannot be adequately identified nor can they be used to predict the behavior of the member within the schismatic dance.

41. Zuckerman, *Strife*. Zuckerman's study is the lengthiest and most detailed treatment of the process of schism that has been written to date and so will figure quite prominently throughout the remainder of our study.

in communal worship.[42] These controversial actions moved some in the congregation to explore more traditional Jewish practices, initiating a process that led this group to embrace Orthodox Judaism and to daven (pray) separately from the rest of the congregation, but still within the facilities of Temple Am Israel. Tensions mounted, but the two groups were able to coexist, even if uneasily, until the Orthodox faction began to use a *mechitza*[43] in their services. A faction within the congregation strongly opposed the use of the *mechitza* on Temple property, based on principles of gender equality and inclusivity.[44] This opposition precipitated the departure of the Orthodox group to establish their own synagogue.

In examining the root causes of the schism in Temple Am Israel, Zuckerman confesses that he expected to find some underlying social cause for the schism congruent with Neibuhr's thesis, and engages in a rehearsal of past research that supported his expectation.[45] However, he was able to find no such underlying cause. The two sides were split quite evenly in all socio-economic categories that have traditionally been associated with motivation to schism: ethnicity (there were converts on both sides), socio-economic status, education, etc. Zuckerman did find some indication that the quality of relationship with Rabbi Kohner tended to be an indicator of factional affiliation; those with good relationships tended to side with Kohner and those who remained in Temple Am Israel, while those with poor relationships tended to defect and align themselves with Bayt Emmett, the new Orthodox synagogue. However, this rule did not apply across the board and served as an accurate predictor in only a limited number of cases. His conclusions regarding motivation for schism are twofold and significant: (1) relationship with the religious leader can serve as motivation for religious schism. Antipathy toward the religious leader may in itself

---

42. A full explanation of the beliefs and practices of Reconstructionist Judaism is not possible here (for a detailed treatment, see Staub, "Reconstructionist Judaism," 2247–60), but a few salient points may be made here. The organization/movement is based upon the teachings of Rabbi Mordecai Kaplan and understands Judaism as an ever-evolving entity that shapes and is shaped by the world around it. It does not view Torah as literally the revealed word of God and does not understand rabbinic law as binding for modern Jews. It has a high stress on gender inclusiveness and has a willingness to adapt liturgical practice to changing times, and so feels no compunction against altering traditional Jewish liturgy, such as the *Amidah* and *Shema*, to be more gender inclusive.

43. A *mechitza* is a type of partition used to divide separate male and female worshippers in more traditional Jewish worship services.

44. Zuckerman, *Strife*, 178–80.

45. Ibid., 91–92, 218–21.

be enough to prompt opposition severe enough to lead to schism. (2) Social factors may be completely absent in schism, which indicates that some schisms are indeed the product of genuine ideological disagreement.[46]

My conclusion here is that schism may be motivated by a variety of factors. The traditional approach, that schism is motivated by socio-economic factors, is not disproved by the work of Doherty and Zuckerman. Rather, it is modified to include social relationship with the religious leader and raw ambition, as well as allowing for ideological motivations absent any directly observable social factors. Therefore I would argue that it is advisable to allow for a spectrum of possible motivations, and possibly, perhaps probably, a combination of motivations when studying schismatic groups.

Propensity to Schism

The fact that a faction within a group is motivated to separate itself does not necessarily mean that this separation will indeed occur, or that it will occur successfully. Indeed, coupled with the faction's motivation for schism are structural considerations that can help to predict the likelihood that a schism will in fact occur when a faction is motivated to separate itself. Along with these structural conditions, schism is more likely to occur successfully during certain developmental stages within the group.

From a structural standpoint, Wilson has suggested that centralization of power is an important "structural determinant of schism. It is suggested that schism is more likely, not so much where a movement is highly decentralized, but where a movement falls at either extreme end of this continuum."[47]

Gamson devotes a brief portion of his study of social protest movements to factionalism and schism, modifying Wilson's proposal. He adopts Niebuhr's theory of the socio-economic motivations for schism, but argues that schism will only occur if the heterogeneous group "lacks adequate mechanisms for managing internal conflict."[48] From a structural standpoint, Gamson argues that groups with a high degree of centralization in their power structures display a lower propensity to schism than do those

---

46. With the caveat noted above that ideology is not formed in a social vacuum.

47. Wilson, "The Sociology of Schism," 10–11.

48. Gamson, *The Strategy of Social Protest*, 103. Gamson makes the argument that schism is sometimes helped along by outside groups who have a vested interest in the schism of a movement. One is reminded somewhat of Gal 2:12.

groups with a low degree of centralization. Indeed, Gamson's research indicates that decentralized movements are more than twice as likely to experience schism as are those that are highly centralized.[49]

Nyomarkay's study of factionalism within the Nazi Party is significant for schismatic studies inasmuch as it represents the first systematic and extensive attempt to explain why factionalism may or may not lead to schism within a group. His basic proposition is that

> the nature or character of intragroup conflicts is intimately and directly related to the nature and character of the group itself. The nature of the group, that is, the nature of its cohesive forces, conditions the nature of the relations within the group and in turn the nature of internal conflicts and their resolution. Hence, the differences in factional behavior are ultimately owing to differences in the nature of groups, specifically to differences in the focus of group cohesion.[50]

More specifically, Nyomarkay draws an intentional contrast between the Nazi Party and its contemporary, the Communist Party of the Soviet Union (CPSU), arguing that the former represents charismatic legitimation[51] and the latter ideological legitimation.[52]

---

49. Ibid., 104. In addition, Gamson (107) notes that, in contrary fashion, decentralized movements with a high degree of bureaucracy are somewhat more likely to experience schism than are decentralized movements with a low degree of bureaucracy.

50. Nyomarkay, *Charisma and Factionalism in the Nazi Party*, 4.

51. Legitimation/legitimacy is of great importance to schismatic studies, and yet a formal definition of legitimation is not forthcoming, even as it relates to the broader field of the sociology and anthropology of religious and political movements. Nyomarkay, *Charisma and Factionalism*, 9–10, "defines" legitimacy by reciting Weber's three means of obtaining legitimacy, which, while helpful, does not actually provide us with a true working definition of legitimacy. At its most basic level, whether we are speaking of religious or political movements, schismatic or otherwise, we might define legitimacy as the validation of a movement's authority to act upon its beliefs. The concept of legitimacy is deserving of full treatment, and it will receive such treatment below. However, its importance is evidenced by the fact that it must be touched upon in discussing the motivation for and propensity to schism, which we will treat prior to our fuller treatment of legitimacy. This all too brief discussion will serve as the basis for our understanding of legitimacy as it is included in our discussion of the motivation and propensity to schism. With specific reference to charismatic and ideological legitimacy, the former is legitimacy derived from the personal appeal of the leader, while the latter is founded upon a system of ideas and adherence to it.

52. Contrary to the evaluation of Wallis, *Salvation and Protest*, 181, Nyomarkay is not arguing for an absolute distinction between charismatic and ideological legitimation. Nyomarkay (147) acknowledges that Stalin, though ideologically legitimated, began to

In contrast to ideologically legitimated groups and their leaders who must define themselves precisely in relation to the accepted ideology, charismatic leaders adopt a more nebulous *weltanschauung*, or "Idea," with which they are synonymous. Not only are the two synonymous, but the charismatic leader comes to be thought of as the embodiment of the *weltanschauung* such that the two cannot be separated.[53] In this way the charismatic leader establishes a single source of legitimation, the *weltanschauung*, and only one individual, the charismatic leader, has access to it.[54] All others within the group must derive their legitimacy from the charismatic leader him/herself, so that their legitimacy is of a secondary and derivative nature.[55] Such a structural arrangement makes successful, or even attempted, schism unlikely.

Despite the fact that successful schism within such a structure is itself unlikely, factionalism tends to run high. In the case of Hitler's leadership of the Nazi Party, factionalism was not suppressed, but rather encouraged. The reasons for this are twofold: (1) the factionalism is itself a byproduct of the charismatic leader's attempt to appeal to as broad an audience as possible, thus amassing a highly heterogeneous following that is inclined toward factionalism.[56] (2) The charismatic leader encourages the factions

---

use "Hitlerian tactics" against his opponents, thus demonstrating characteristics of charismatic leadership. In this way, Nyomarkay actually implies a spectrum of means of legitimation, with the purely charismatic and the purely ideological lying at either extreme, with the possibility of overlapping characteristics of each in the middle. His juxtaposition of charisma and ideology as means of legitimation here seems to be a heuristic tool. For obvious reasons, his treatment of charismatic legitimation here is much better developed than that of the ideological, and so it will be necessary at times to infer an evaluation of ideological legitimation.

53. Nyomarkay, *Nazi Party*, 22: "The term 'leader' implies by definition the personification of a Weltanschauung. A Weltanschauung, in turn, is created by a man of spiritual force and imagination who has been chosen by Destiny to bring it down to earth. A Weltanschauung is not so much an objective entity or a logical construct, but the subjective experience of a man who believes himself called upon to transmit this spiritual conception to the rest of mankind [sic]."

54. Ibid., 21, describes the relationship between leader and idea thusly: "The charismatic leader is not the interpreter of an ideology, but the discoverer of an idea."

55. Ibid., 4–5: "The task of factions is to attain legitimacy by identifying themselves with the source of authority. Should a faction fail in this endeavor, the members of the group will regard it as illegitimate, and it will either wither away for lack of support or split the movement and establish itself as an independent group . . . Consequently, Hitler remained above factional conflicts that took place on the secondary levels of leadership and thereby ensured the unity of the movement against the danger of factional splits."

56. Several historical vignettes are scattered throughout *Nazi Party* that illustrate

to compete with one another in order to enhance the leader's charismatic status.⁵⁷ This second point merits further development since it provides a window into the inner life of such a group.

The successful charismatic leader will maintain a high level of abstraction regarding the nature of the *weltanschauung* because (1) such a level of abstraction again allows for a wider appeal and, more importantly, (2) precise definition will entail a limitation of the charismatic leader's absolute authority. Nyomarkay's remarks on this subject are worth noting here:

> A program which is more than an opportunistic tool in the hands of the leader is by definition incompatible with absolute leadership. Such a program becomes organically related to the goals of the movement and thus becomes ideological; as such, it binds the leader to certain courses of action and may be used as a standard to evaluate the leader's actions. An ideological program gives every member of the political party an opportunity (if not an obligation) to judge the actions of the leader and to call him to account.⁵⁸

If the *weltanschauung* remains relatively undefined the charismatic leader can adapt it to fit his or her immediate needs. Expediency in maintaining the leader's place of prestige trumps any ideological considerations. The vagueness of the *weltanschauung* allows followers to interpret both it and the leader according to their own needs and desires, leading to a variety of groups and interpretations within the heterogeneous movement. In turn, these factions seek to gain the leader's approval of their interpretation of him or her and the *weltanschauung*, since the leader's approval supplies the faction with derivative legitimacy. In order to maintain her or his status, the charismatic leader will strive to maintain these competing perceptions as long as possible. Inevitably, factions with competing interpretations will come into conflict with one another; in this situation, the charismatic leader will defer for as long as possible any decision that would validate one side over the other.

As the conflict escalates, the leader must eventually intervene, but not as triumphing and vindictive conqueror. Rather, he or she intervenes

---

the fact that the amorphous nature of the *Weltanschauung* not only allowed for but encouraged the inclusion of a variety of ideological orientations. One such example can be found on ibid., 92–93, in which Hitler shifts political course from a leftist socialist direction toward a more right-wing stance that allowed for the inclusion of right-wing conservatives and capitalistic industrialists.

57. Nyomarkay, *Nazi Party*, 46.
58. Ibid., 86.

as arbiter, "correcting" but not punishing the party with whom he or she disagrees.[59] In fact, the leader(s) of the losing faction are often placated by having a higher position within the group conferred upon them.[60] This immediately strikes one as counter-intuitive, but it is in accordance with the charismatic leader's ultimate goal. The charismatic leader is not so concerned with agreement on points of ideology, but in having her or his followers confirm her or his charismatic status. Additionally, the charismatic leader, by playing the role of peace-making arbiter, enhances her or his status by reinforcing the perception that only the charismatic leader is able to step in and broker between two disagreeing sides.

As noted above, Nyomarkay offers little by way of describing the processes that occur within an ideological movement. This is not a criticism since these are not the questions to which he addresses himself in his study. However, it is helpful for this study to learn something more of the processes within an ideological movement, and perhaps a few insights into these processes may be deduced from what Nyomarkay has said about charismatic movements. We must first of all note that Nyomarkay's juxtaposition of charismatic and ideological movements is not absolute; as we will see below, successful schism, whether it be of a charismatic or ideological nature, is more often than not dependent upon a charismatic figure around whom an exit group can form and "talk themselves out of" the parent group. In the case of the CPSU, we might view Lenin as the charismatic figure around whom an ideological movement coalesced. Secondly, if charismatic movements have high tolerance for faction and low levels of schism, it would stand to reason that ideological movements have a low tolerance for faction and a high level of schism, and our examination of Wallis's work will bear this out shortly. The low tolerance for faction derives from the fact that the center of the movement is not an individual who embodies an amorphous Idea, but a well-defined ideology that has an existence distinct from any one person or group. The ideology must be implemented, and must be

59. Again, the disagreement of the leader with one of the factions is not motivated by an ideological position, but out of a desire to maintain his or her charismatic status. The leader will usually side for the faction that best maintains his or her status.

60. As a result of the northern faction of the party openly contradicting Hitler on the subject of expropriation, Hitler convened the Bamberg conference and censured the faction without punishment and no resignations were required or voluntarily offered by the leaders of the faction. Gregor Strasser, the leader of the faction was immediately promoted and, some months later, Josef Goebbels, a secondary leader in the northern faction, was also promoted to district leader of Berlin-Brandenburg. Nyomarkay, *Nazi Party*, 89.

interpreted in order to be implemented; the need for interpretation leads (post-modern and reader-response critics might say, "inevitably leads") to differences of interpretation and from there to factions. Because standing within the group is predicated upon ideological orthodoxy rather than the approval of a charismatic leader, there is a low level of toleration for differing interpretations. Unlike the charismatic movement, ideological movements can show a propensity toward harsh reactions against factions that are deemed ideologically unorthodox.[61]

Wallis recognizes the value and validity of Nyomarkay's research inasmuch as it "begins systematically to raise the issue of schism in a new way; to reorient the problem from the question of why schisms occur, to that of accounting for the differential propensity to schism of different movements."[62] However, he also recognizes the inability of Nyomarkay's conceptualization to deal fully with the very questions he has raised.[63] Therefore, Wallis sets out to, and indeed does, provide a more thoroughgoing model of the propensity to schism, integrating, modifying, and confirming the work of Nyomarkay.

Wallis argues that schism occurs when a schismatic leader is able to secure a portion of a movement's membership and convince them to break away from the movement. In order to convince them to break away, the leader must be able to legitimate her/himself.[64] In order to legitimate her/himself, means of legitimation must be available to the schismatic leader. Therefore, it is the availability of the means of legitimation that ultimately determines whether or not a motivated faction within a movement will be able to successfully break away.[65]

61. A prime example is the hunting down and assassination of Leon Trotsky. See Gamson, *Strategy*, 100.

62. Wallis, *Salvation and Protest*, 180–81.

63. Ibid., 180–81.

64. The topic of legitimacy and legitimation is one that is of great importance to the subject of schism and could very easily be treated as a separate and distinct topic within the model that we are constructing. However, given that legitimacy is such a pervasive theme, appearing in every component of our model, we will discuss different aspects of legitimacy as they apply to the component being addressed. Legitimation may be defined as "a process through which a social system or some aspect of it comes to be accepted as appropriate and generally supported by those who participate in it. Since it is difficult to hold a system together through coercion for long periods, the most effective way to maintain social cohesion is for people to believe in and accept the system as it is" (*s.v.* "Legitimation," in Johnson, *The Blackwell Dictionary of Sociology*, 156).

65. Wallis, *Salvation and Protest*, 181.

Wallis classifies the means of legitimation available to the schismatic leader into two distinct groups: (1) alternative means of legitimation, and (2) the same means of legitimation.[66] Wallis illustrates the former in a very roundabout way, citing Zald and Ash, who in turn cite Miller.[67] The use of alternative means of legitimation, in Miller's example, is illustrated by the Montanists, Feeneyites, and Saint Francis of Assisi. Miller argues that these representative sects either remained within or separated from the Roman Catholic Church dependent upon their ability to accept "the ultimate authority of the Word as revealed in the Bible, and interpreted by the Fathers of the Church, versus the word of contemporary church authorities."[68] In this scenario, schism depends upon the willingness of the factions to accept alternative means of legitimation since traditional means did not lend support to their particular ideology. In the cases of the Montanists and Feeneyites, alternative means of legitimation were ultimately accepted by these factions and schism occurred. In the case of Saint Francis, submission was given to traditional means of legitimation employed by the Church, and so he remained within it.[69]

In contrast to the alternative means of legitimation, which must be essentially *manufactured* by the schismatic group, the same or traditional means of legitimation must be *available* to factional groups if they are to successfully employ them for the purpose of separating from the parent group. Indeed, the remainder of the first half of Wallis's theory is based upon the availability of traditional means of legitimation as an indicator of the likelihood of schism within a movement.

Before proceeding with the development of his model, however, Wallis finds it necessary to address the fact that extremist movements tend to have a higher incidence of schism in contrast to conventional religious and political organizations. Zald and Ash understand this phenomenon in terms of inclusive and exclusive groups. Inclusive groups are identified by their "looser criteria of affiliation and of doctrinal orthodoxy," and these relaxed positions make them "split-resistant," presumably because it allows them to

---

66. Ibid., 181–82.

67. Ibid.; Zald and Ash, "Social Movement Organizations," 337; Miller, "Formal Organization and Schismogenesis."

68. Zald and Ash, "Social Movement Organizations," 337.

69. If there is a flaw in Wallis's overall theory, it is that he leaves this important aspect of the schismatic process underdeveloped. While he goes to great pains to develop his theory of the availability of the same means of legitimation, he says virtually nothing here about the process by which schismatic groups develop alternative means of legitimation.

tolerate a high degree of heterogeneity and disagreement.[70] Conversely, the exclusive group "spews . . . forth" its dissidents.[71] Nyomarkay, on the other hand, labels groups as totalitarian or non-totalitarian, arguing that, "In a non-totalitarian group the principle of legitimacy is pluralistic –i.e. based on segmental participation—and factions can exist without destroying the group. In a totalitarian movement the principle of legitimacy is monistic—i.e. based on an almost total identification—and factions can exist only if they do not attack the principle of legitimacy."[72] The difficulty with these two proposals, argues Wallis, is that they cannot be exactly equated. "The totalitarian movement may have stringent criteria of doctrinal orthodoxy but rather loose criteria of affiliation: the Catholic Church in the Middle Ages, for example."[73]

As an alternative, Wallis proposes that we think in terms of uniquely and pluralistically legitimate groups. The uniquely legitimate groups "will tend to define the boundaries of doctrine rather sharply to distinguish themselves from those beliefs and programmes which they reject," while pluralistically legitimate groups "do not completely reject the validity of alternative paths to truth, salvation, or utopia."[74] Wallis is quick to clarify that there are different kinds of uniquely legitimate movements, and the social status of such movements is of immediate importance to addressing the question of propensity to schism. The attainment of power within society puts at the group's disposal the means of suppressing factionalism within its ranks, thereby minimizing or at least reducing the likelihood of schism.[75]

---

70. Zald and Ash, "Social Movement Organizations," 337.

71. Ibid..

72. Nyomarkay, *Nazi Party*, 150.

73. Wallis, *Salvation and Protest*, 182. We should also note here that it may be more prudent to understand Wallis's pluralistically/unique distinction as being the extreme ends of a spectrum rather than an either/or dichotomy. Few groups could be unquestionably defined as one or the other. Further, we may be able to apply the pluralistically/unique concept to certain *aspects* of a movement's beliefs. Controversies over some aspects of a movement's beliefs may be tolerated if the beliefs are more peripheral to the movement's identity, while little or no tolerance for questioning might be exhibited regarding central beliefs.

74. Ibid., 183.

75. Ibid. Again, Wallis does not provide us with detailed analysis of this type of group. However, since the focus here is on propensity to schism, and uniquely legitimate groups that have attained power within society are less likely to experience schism, such groups fall outside the scope of Wallis's concern. Additionally, such an omission does not impact our present study since it is almost certain that the Johannine community occupied a

Generally, however, the pluralistically legitimate group, with its openness to the legitimacy of other groups, has a lower propensity to schism given that its members are willing to tolerate greater degrees of ideological diversity. The uniquely legitimate group, on the other hand, will demonstrate a low tolerance for disagreement with the group's accepted doctrine and therefore has a higher propensity to schism. The uniquely legitimate group then becomes the focus for Wallis's further analysis.

In order to predict the likelihood that schism will occur within a uniquely legitimate movement, Wallis works out a formula in which the means of legitimation adopted by the movement correspond with the availability of these means to the members of the movement in order to arrive at increasing levels of propensity to schism. Wallis illustrates his conclusions in the following chart.[76]

		Means of Legitimation	
		Singular	Plural
	One	1	4
Availability	Few (i.e. an elite)	2	5
	Many	3	6

In this formula, the increasing digits correspond to an increasing likelihood that schism will occur within the uniquely legitimate group. In (1), where we have only one means of legitimation and it is available to only one member of the group, much like our examination of Hitler's charismatic leadership within the Nazi Party, schism is most unlikely, as the example of Hitler indeed demonstrated. On the other hand, (6), where multiple means of legitimation are available to multiple members of the movement, schism is most likely to occur. Illustrative of this is the Pentecostal movement, within which "the principal basis of legitimation is by means of the charismata of possession by the Holy Spirit. Since the experience of being filled with the Spirit is theoretically available to all born-again believers, this means of legitimating challenges to authority is widely available."[77]

It is important to note that Wallis's theory of the propensity to schism does not contradict or negate any of the previously proposed methods of

---

place of marginality rather than power in the society in which it existed.

76. Ibid., 184.

77. Ibid., 185.

predicting the likelihood of schism. On the contrary, these other proposals become subsumed under Wallis's more expansive treatment of the subject. Thus, Wallis gives us a general heuristic device by which to examine schismatic groups and the others provide categories for understanding the specific type of schismatic group with which we are dealing. But, as noted above, Wallis argues that propensity to schism depends upon structural aspects of a movement as well as particular developmental stages of movements. To the latter we now turn.

In addition to the proper structural conditions, Wallis argues that successful schism is dependent upon the appropriate timing of the schism. More specifically, Wallis isolates two particular developmental periods in the life of a movement that offer opportune moments for schism: (1) the early, developmental stages of a movement, and (2) the death of the movement's leader. Both periods, Wallis argues, are periods of instability in a movement's authority structure.

Early in a movement's development, several factors combine to make schism a very real possibility. (1) Authority has not been or has been poorly institutionalized, with the result that authority "remains a fluid property scarcely trammelled (*sic*) by routine."[78] If leadership is charismatic, there has not been sufficient time for the movement to crystallize around the charismatic leader, and leadership and organizational positions are more or less vacant in less or non-charismatic movements. Further, the leadership institutions that are in place have not been fully tested so as to define the extent of leadership's authority.[79] (2) The concept of legitimation held by incoming members of the new movement may not match the means of legitimation adopted by the movement, thereby eliciting a challenge to the authority of the movement.[80]

---

78. Ibid., 187.

79. Ibid. We might additionally note that some groups make a conscious effort to maintain such undefined power structures beyond the initial phases of the movement's development. Doherty, *Hicksite*, 22, notes that the Quaker movement intentionally maintained a loose organization that was based upon precedent. "Since the Society was not tightly organized, precise relationships among different bodies were not defined. Thus, for example, methods of appointment and problems of jurisdiction could easily become the subject of controversy." In this way Wallis's proposal is qualified: the structural conditions that Wallis associates with a particular phase in a movement's development may actually be maintained beyond this phase, thereby making schism possible long after the movement has passed this particular stage in its development.

80. Ibid. This is particularly problematic in the early stages of a sect's development because converts tend to enter in large numbers, sometimes even in pre-existing groups.

While authority structures are unstable in the early phases of a movement's development, they can be destabilized by the death of a charismatic leader.[81] This destabilization can be minimized by advance preparations for the transfer of power, but even this type of foresight is not a guaranteed prophylactic against internecine fighting over succession, which can result in schism.[82] Given that infighting and schism can occur within a movement that has prepared itself for the death of its charismatic leader, it should not come to us as a surprise that this type of conflict is all the more likely when there is no heir-apparent, or, even worse, when there are multiple claimants to the position of leadership.[83]

It should also be noted here that Wallis does not argue that the death of the prophet means the inevitable dissolution of the movement, only that it is an opportune time for the alienated to separate themselves from the movement. A common assumption in earlier anthropological and sociological studies of charismatic cults was that the death of the charismatic leader was also the death knell for the cult. The conclusion of J. Milton Yinger that a cult "tends to be small, to break up easily, and is relatively unlikely to develop into an established sect or a denomination,"[84] both reflected the scholarly consensus of the time and continued to impact sociological and anthropological studies of cults for some time. This position has fallen into disrepute, however. Wallis himself implies that groups do indeed survive the death of the charismatic leader, even if it does present an opportune time for the alienated to separate. More recently, J. Gordon Melton has summarized the growing opposition to Yinger's position and Melton himself also rejects it.[85]

The larger numbers of converts make it more likely that disaffected groups will form and split away. Wallis also notes that the incongruence of the concepts of legitimation held by the movement and incoming members does not cease with the consolidation of the movement's leadership. Rather, this phenomenon continues, but on an *individual* basis. Single new members choose to leave the movement over legitimacy concerns, but the movement is well-enough established to prevent the formation of groups of malcontents, unlike in the early stages of development.

81. Ibid., 188.

82. Ibid., 188–89, notes the case of the succession of Mary Baker Eddy within the Christian Science movement as an example of infighting within a movement in spite of careful advance preparation for the transfer of power.

83. Ibid., 189.

84. *Religion, Society, and the Individual*, 154.

85. "Introduction: When Prophets Die," 1–4.

It ought also to be noted that Wallis's assertion regarding the death of the charismatic leader as prime time for schism has not gone unchallenged. J. R. Lewis argues that social consensus is the "real glue that maintains the plausibility of any given worldview...."[86] Therefore, it is the breakdown of social consensus within the group, not the death of the charismatic leader, that leads to schism. However, Lewis's study focuses strictly on new religious movements within American Indian cultures extending from the late eighteenth to the late nineteenth century, and certain common features of the different movements ought to be noted. (1) The various groups are ethnically homogeneous. All of the groups under consideration are American Indian and many of the movements are confined to particular tribes.[87] Other movements, such as the Ghost Dance movement of ca. 1890, may extend beyond customary tribal boundaries, but they are adapted to specific tribal customs.[88] (2) These new religious movements tended to spring up among the American Indians as a reaction to colonization by European and American powers. (3) The American Indian tribes that contributed to these various movements also tended to be "demoralized" by colonial oppression, with high rates of alcoholism and suicide evident among the populace.[89] In other words, these groups were highly homogeneous, in contrast to the heterogeneous groups that we have seen involved in schism. This may at first seem to confirm Lewis' criticism of Wallis's theory: it is not the death of the charismatic leader that causes the schism. Rather, it is the social cohesion of the group or lack thereof that causes schism. However, a closer examination of the information reveals that Lewis' proposal clarifies Wallis's rather than negating it. Wallis proposes that the death of the charismatic leader marks a *phase* within the life of a group during which schism is more likely to occur. If the group is homogeneous, they have connections other than the charismatic leader that hold them together. On the other hand, if the group is heterogeneous, the charismatic leader's death allows for the surfacing of the differences within the group, thus making schism more likely to occur.

Wallis's categories for the stages of a sect's life in which schism is more likely to occur are helpful, but they do not exhaust the possibilities. The

86. Lewis, "American Indian Prophets," 47–57.
87. For example, Handsome Lake's religious movement among the Iroquois. Ibid., 53.
88. Ibid., 54.
89. Ibid., 48.

shortcoming in Wallis's categorization is that it focuses on the *predictable* phases of a sect's life cycle, but do not broaden out to include other *possible* phases. Other *possible* phases which could lead to schism are, of course, innumerable and to expect that Wallis's model would cover all the possibilities would be nit-picking in the extreme. However, some of these possibilities do happen often enough that they warrant inclusion in our discussion. We will focus here specifically on two that can be illustrated well by the literature.[90]

Zuckerman, in his study of schism in a contemporary synagogue in the Pacific Northwest, focuses on the question of motivation for schism, as we have noted above. As such, he does not address himself directly to the question of propensity to schism, i.e., what structural and developmental conditions within the synagogue allowed for the schism? However, he does

---

90. We ought also to note the categories established by Baer, *Utopia*, 26, for classifying the schisms that have occurred within LDS: (1) the assassination of Joseph Smith (2) the repudiation of polygamy, and (3) the Great Depression. These categories are significant in that they confirm one aspect of Wallis's theory, and anticipate two additional stages drawn from Doherty and Zuckerman. The death of Joseph Smith and the resulting schisms within LDS confirm Wallis's assertion that the death of the prophet often precipitates schism within a movement. As a matter of fact, the death of Smith and the succession struggles that ensued are quite often used as textbook examples of the difficulties that arise within a movement after the death of the prophet or charismatic leader. Likewise, the fact that the Great Depression precipitated a large number of schisms within LDS (as well as many other religious groups of the time) confirms what we will see in Doherty's work, namely, that times of economic hardship are also prime times for schism. Baer's third point, the abandonment of polygamy as a time of schism, confirms that, very often, schism occurs because a faction with the larger group begins to feel that the group is abandoning its identity, causing an ideological dispute within the group. In the case of LDS, polygamy is not merely a cultural practice necessitated by high numbers of female members and lower numbers of male members. Rather, important theological significance was attached to polygamy in the early stages of the movement. It was believed, and is still believed by many fundamentalist Mormons, that a higher status in the afterlife is accorded the man who produces more children through multiple marriages. The official abandonment of polygamy by LDS led many within the movement to believe that the leadership of the movement was willing to compromise with the "Gentile" world in order to avoid continued persecution. In the case of LDS, the situation cannot be described as purely ideological given that lower economic standing seems to have contributed to the need of these fundamentalists to ensure their better standing in the afterlife through polygamy. However, the fact that the theological benefit of polygamy is deferred to the afterlife undercuts the argument that this is a purely socioeconomic issue. Stark and Bainbridge, *The Future of Religion*, 103, note that such other-worldly compensation for present misery is not uncommon in religious movements: "For people who are poor, the most effective compensators define material goods as of little value in comparison to heavenly bliss: self-denial on earth buys riches in the world to come."

give us information that can provide insight into the possible structural and developmental reasons for schism. Zuckerman describes the membership of Temple Am Israel as limited in size during the 1950s and 1960s, experiencing moderate growth in the 1970s, but then booming in membership during the 1980s, leading up to the split in the early 1990s. The connection between the growth of a movement or body and subsequent split is not accidental. As Zuckerman amusingly puts it, "Mother Growth inevitably gave birth to Baby Cliques."[91] Indeed, the formation of "cliques" or factions within the larger group is symptomatic of the increasing heterogeneity of the larger group. Zuckerman testifies to the increasingly heterogeneous character of Temple Am Israel and notes that Rabbi Moishe Kohner adopted a policy of attempting to make a variety of approaches to Judaism (Conservative, Reform, and Renewal) work within the single congregation of Temple Am Israel.[92] Marcello Bergman, a member of Temple Am Israel at the time, positively sums up the ethos of Rabbi Kohner's approach and the resulting climate engendered:

> What happened is that Rabbi Moishe enabled anybody who wanted to affiliate with Temple Am Israel to affiliate, regardless of their level of *yiddishkeit*. I mean, assuming they were Jewish—and in some cases even there he had many ceremonies and many ways of inviting non-Jewish partners of Jews into the synagogue. So it was a very big tent.[93]

On the other hand, the heterogeneity that was being actively promoted by Rabbi Kohner was not seen as a positive by all members of the congregation. Bruce Wallin represents a different take on the heterogeneity that accompanied Temple Am Israel's growth:

> Homosexuality was just one issue in the whole multicultural-Native-American-racism-lesbian—uh—diversity . . . it was a joke. It just became a joke. That if there was any kind of leftist political trend going on, you could be sure that Temple Am Israel—you know what side Temple Am Israel would be on . . . . It was like a 'Saturday Night Live' routine, like a comedy—it was a parody.[94]

---

91. Zuckerman, *Strife*, 102.
92. Ibid., 77.
93. Ibid., 79.
94. Ibid., 110.

Elsewhere, Wallin describes the process that led up to the schism: "Various things happened . . . that led me to become alienated."[95] Wallin's remarks are particularly revealing in that they allow us to articulate a three step process by which growth of the movement can lead to its fragmentation. Wallin's characterization of his feeling within the group as "alienation" is telling, and reflects some of Doherty's work, cited above. Growth can lead to heterogeneity within the movement, which can lead some within the movement to feel that the movement has lost its identity, or that their own views, at least, no longer match well with the views of the movement. The resulting sense of alienation can ultimately lead to schism. M. Leatham sees such growth as "a variable of importance in many instances, one that must be seen in terms of whether a fundamental identity shift is perceived by one or both of the parties."[96]

In addition to the rapid growth of a movement, socioeconomic pressures exerted from outside the community may also contribute to a sense of alienation which leads to schism. Doherty notes that the beginnings of the Hicksite controversy in the Society of Friends can be traced to 1815, a year that would come to be defined by later historiographers as a watershed year for the United States.[97] The emerging Industrial Revolution began to bring about significant changes in the economy of the young nation, which resulted in a corresponding destabilization of a society that had maintained a significant degree of stability throughout the eighteenth century.[98] These changes tended to result in a growing disparity between the wealthier urban Friends and the less wealthy rural and urban-artisan Friends.[99] As noted above in our treatment of Doherty's theory of motivation for schism, socioeconomic changes can lead some within a group to reevaluate the group's isolationist attitude toward the outside world, thereby adopting a more positive stance toward interaction with the outside world which

95. Ibid., 95.

96. Leatham, personal correspondence, July 25, 2008.

97. Doherty, *Hicksite*, 24.

98. Ibid., 23. It may seem a bit surprising that Doherty would describe the century that saw both the American and French Revolutions as "stable." However, he refers here primarily to the means by which one attains material wealth and status, which remained relatively unchanged in the United States after the Revolution.

99. Ibid., 51–89. This section is composed of three chapters. The first two chapters are spent, in large part, in carefully attempting to reconstruct the economic changes occurring among the rural and urban Friends, with a third chapter spent detailing the Hicksite/rural response to the increasing wealth and assimilation of the urban Friends.

necessitates adjustment in the beliefs espoused by the group. Such a move will often, if not usually, elicit a negative reaction from others within the group who believe that such a shift represents an unacceptable compromise with the outside world. The ultimate question, as with that of numerical growth within a movement, is one of identity. However, as illustrated by the Hicksite controversy, the struggle over the identity of the movement arises not because of an influx of heterogeneous groups into the movement, but because of exterior socioeconomic pressures being placed upon the movement and so forcing a response.

To summarize, we may gauge the propensity of a faction to successfully split away from the parent group by examining the parent group structurally and developmentally. We should note first that schism tends to occur within a group that is uniquely rather than pluralistically legitimate. Groups that allow for the fact that they are not the sole possessors of legitimacy tend to be able to tolerate a higher degree of heterogeneity when compared to those groups that see themselves as possessing the only true means of legitimation, be these means one or several. The ability of a faction within a uniquely legitimate group to split away depends in large part on its ability to appropriate for itself the means to legitimate its claims to authority. Groups which limit the means of legitimation to a few and limit access to these means to only a few within the movement tend to have lower incidences of schism, while those groups who allow broad access to a multiplicity of legitimating institutions and structures tend to have a higher incidence of schism. However, a group may demonstrate a willingness to adopt alternative means of legitimation, in which case we will usually find a charismatic leader who advocates for this alternative means of legitimation and around whom the faction crystallizes.

In addition, certain phases in the life of a movement can be shown to be more conducive to schism and it is usually during these times that successful schism will occur. Of the phases within the life of a movement that are predictable, the earliest phase of development, in which authority structures and legitimating institutions have not been fully developed, and the period immediately following the death of the movement's leader are the occasions when schism is most likely to occur successfully. On the other hand, phases in which schism can successfully occur are not always predictable. Most notable among these are those times when the movement experiences rapid and substantial growth, which allows for an increasingly high degree of heterogeneity within the movement, and times of socioeconomic pressure.

The Polemics of Schism

Schismatic polemics tend to follow a rather predictable as well as functional script in the schismatic "dance." Schismatic polemics start out negatively, but mildly, usually beginning in the exit group stage of the dance, but carrying over into the post-separation phase of the schism. As the process of schism progresses the rhetoric increases in negativity as each side becomes more entrenched in its critical evaluation of the other. Thus we find that, as the schismatic process reaches its breaking point, the rhetoric tends to become extremely harsh and the opponents are depicted as having no positive or redeeming qualities. This escalating rhetoric helps to solidify group identity by firmly asserting the rightness of the "in group" and the wrongness of the "out group," and not only their wrongness but the reprehensible nature of their beliefs. In addition, the polemical language can be broken down into several types of polemical speech: rhetorical attempts to undermine one another's legitimacy claims, attempts to cast their opponents as unfaithful to the movement's beliefs and traditions, impugning one another's morality, the use of negative symbolic terms to label one another, and describing one another in terms that tend toward dehumanization.

It should be noted that the intensity of the polemic directed against the schismatic group by the parent group is often a good indicator of the size or prominence of the schismatic group. In Rochford's study of a small schism within the Hare Krishna movement in Los Angeles, the size of the schismatic group, the Conch Club, relative to the parent group, ISKCON,[100] was very small and their standing within the group was mid-level. Therefore, the Club did not draw any great deal of ire from ISKCON when they separated.[101] The split in Temple Am Israel reflects a different situation. While Bayt Emmett represented a minority within the Temple, they were a substantial minority and held high status within the group. The resulting

---

100. International Society for Krishna CONsciouness, an organization begun in the 1960s to promote Krishna Consciouness.

101. Rochford, "Factionalism," 171, notes that a number of still-committed but wavering ISKCON members attended the Conch Club's "Kirtan Hall" meetings. Though they feared a degree of ostracism should they actually join the Club, the ISKCON members held no such misgivings about attending a Kirtan as a visitor.

schism was, as we have seen, highly vitriolic on both sides. In the case of Nueva Jerusalén,[102] the two sides were evenly enough divided that separation was brought about by physical expulsion in which planks, clubs, machetes, and rocks were used by one side to drive the other out of the colony, and at least one building was set fire. Though no deaths were reported, many machete gashes and concussions were.[103] Again, though it is no failsafe method of gauging the prominence of the schismatic group within the parent group, the level of the intensity of the polemical rhetoric can serve as a good indicator of this.

While intensity of expression can tell us something of the size and/or status of the schismatic group within the parent group, the particular form of expression taken in schismatic polemics should not be understood as an objective description of the realities occurring within the schismatic process. Polemics are formulated in a context in which both sides are fighting for the identity, the heart and soul, of the group. Their descriptions of one another are then understandably vitriolic and exaggerated. This becomes ever truer as the schismatic dance progresses and the two sides become more entrenched in their negative evaluations of one another. Not only are the polemical descriptions of the opposing sides of the schism not objective, but they also tend to tell us more about the side producing the polemic than they do about the side toward which they are aimed. The schismatics' polemic against the parent group, in other words, tells us more about the schismatic group itself than it does about the parent group.

Let me move on to some illustrative examples of what we have thus far discussed regarding the nature of schismatic polemics. In the first instance we will attempt to point out examples of most of the classes of polemical speech described above, using the succeeding instances to broaden our understanding of each speech-type. In addition, the perspectival nature of schismatic polemic will be discussed.

Heger argues that the conflicts recorded in Ezra-Nehemiah are indications of "the existence of ideological dissension among the returnees from exile, and likely also between some of the returnees and those who did not go into exile,"[104] and that this ideological dissension manifested itself in "disparate attitudes toward the rebuilding of the Temple, the offering

---

102. See Leatham, "'Shaking out the Mat'" 175–87.

103. Ibid., 183.

104. Heger, *Cult as the Catalyst for Division*, 21–24 represent a summary of Heger's more detailed argument found in *The Three Biblical Altar Laws* 335–50.

of sacrifices and the extension of decrees and prohibitions regarding the Sabbath."[105] The two sides of the debate centered on the high priest and the representative of the kingly line.[106] Heger's proposal regarding the social setting of Ezra-Nehemiah is helpful when examining much of the polemic recorded in Nehemiah.

In Neh 2:19–20, Nehemiah's opponents at first ridicule his efforts at reconstructing the wall of Jerusalem but then shift to charges of rebellion. Nehemiah's response is to assert that God has called him to reconstruct the wall and to deny that they have any claim on Jerusalem. This brief exchange is instructive for understanding the development of our model. At face value, each party is making claims about the other: Nehemiah's opponents argue that he is planning to rebel and Nehemiah retorts that they have no rightful claim to his undertaking. A more careful reading, however, may reveal that Nehemiah, in recording both his opponents' accusations and his

---

105. Ibid., 22.

106. Ibid., 22–24. Heger's argument is somewhat difficult to critique. He labels the cases in his study as schisms arising out of conflicts over cult (1). While he carefully defines cult, he leaves it to the reader to supply a definition of schism. The result is that we do not know if Heger has defined the process as we have, nor do we have a model with which to compare our own. However, Blenkinsopp, *Ezra-Nehemiah*, 68–69, reconstructs the historical situation during this period in way that is favorable toward Heger's understanding, even if their understandings of the situation are not identical. Blenkinsopp argues for several waves of returnees from exile, descendants of the deported Judean aristocracy, who attempt to assert their ownership rights over the lands taken over by the poor of the land after the Babylonian deportations. These social differences soon also found expression within the Temple cult as the higher levels of the priesthood attempted to exert their control over Temple resources. Nehemiah's opposition to their program and his attempt to limit their access to Temple resources, Blenkinsopp argues, would have cast him in a favorable light with the lower Levitical orders. Blenkinsopp sums up the situation by arguing that returnees and their immediate descendants "constituted themselves as a distinct entity within which participation in, and of course active support of, the cult were closely linked with social and economic status in the province. Effective control of the 'redemptive media,' in effect the sacrificial system, translated into social control, including the ability to dictate terms for qualification as members of this entity. *It is this situation more than anything else which created the conditions for the emergence of sectarianism in the Second Temple period*" (69; emphasis mine; see also Blenkinsopp, "A Jewish Sect of the Persian Period," 5–20). While Blenkinsopp's reconstruction does not constitute a proper schism, it does represent a situation in which different factions are in competition with one another and polemicizing against one another in a religious setting. Though Heger and Blenkinsopp differ in the details of the historical setting of Ezra-Nehemiah, the general contours of their reconstruction are similar enough and do represent a conflict within a religious movement that eventually results in a certain degree of fragmentation of the movement. For this reason we will include it in our discussion.

retort, is saying more about his own position than about his opponents'. The charge that Nehemiah is planning to rebel is highly ironic, since we know from chapters 1 and 2 that Nehemiah has not only received the permission of the king in rebuilding the walls of Jerusalem, but his undertaking is actually being financed from the royal coffers. For him to record the accusation of his opponents only serves to highlight his justified actions through their ironic and ill-informed statement. By recording their charge so near his own commissioning by the king, Nehemiah is actually strengthening his claim to be in the right. In other words, Nehemiah is asserting the legitimacy of his mission and the illegitimacy of the Tobiads' opposition to it.

Note also that we cannot verify the historical accuracy of Nehemiah's report. We cannot know if the Tobiads actually made such an accusation. If they did make such an accusation, we cannot know if it formed the core of their dispute with Nehemiah or if it was merely an off-hand comment or the like. If we make certain assumptions about the historicity of the report we can use it to reconstruct the Tobiads' position, but the most certain conclusions we can draw from it have to do with Nehemiah and not his opponents. Secondly, and more obviously, Nehemiah asserts that he has not only kingly sanction, but divine sanction as well. His third assertion, that his opponents have no share in Jerusalem, is telling in that it communicates that Nehemiah sees his own position as enviable; his opponents, after all, have not made any claim to have a share in Jerusalem. By rejecting a claim that his opponents have not even made, he presumes that his opponents actually want to participate in the reconstruction, thus betraying that he sees his work as so important that outsiders would want to participate.[107]

Nehemiah's rhetoric escalates even further in chapter 6 when he begins to claim that his opponents are attempting to take his life. No actual attempt is ever made, nor does he ever see an assassin with a weapon approaching him, yet he claims on at least six occasions his opponents attempt to lure him into a situation in which they can do him in. He concludes the narrative by praying that God would remember their attempted misdeeds.

107. This serves as a nice contrast with 1 John, where the author presents membership in his group as desirable since only through membership in the group can one gain access to God. Contrarily, the fact that the opponents have voluntarily left the group is a patent demonstration of their sinful and reprehensible character. Note also that this sets up an interesting quandary. The author seemingly quotes the opponents as claiming to have no sin, and he refutes this, arguing that they are indeed sinners, even lawless! Yet the only concrete example he offers of their sin is the fact that they left and that they do not love the brothers and sisters, and this lack of love is demonstrated, seemingly, in their defection!

In Neh 13:4-9, Nehemiah recounts that a room had been prepared within the Temple precincts for Tobiah by the high priest while Nehemiah was absent from Jerusalem. Upon returning, Nehemiah became angry, threw out all the furniture, and ordered the room restored to its original function. While no physical violence is ever reported being committed against a person in the narration of Nehemiah's conflicts with his opponents, multiple claims are put forward that such designs were actually made and the angry throwing out of Tobiah's property from the Temple is an indication of the violence that might have occurred had Tobiah had the misfortune of being present upon Nehemiah's return.

In addition, Nehemiah's repeated claims that his opponents are attempting to kill him brings their morality into question. According to Nehemiah's report, they are not only attempting to kill a royal official, but they are attempting to accomplish this end by means of trickery and deceit, even going so far as attempting to kill him within the Temple precincts, thereby demonstrating their "sacrilege."[108] The effect is heightened even further by the fact that Shemaiah has cloaked the conspiracy in the guise of a prophetic oracle.

The language that we find in the beginning stages of Nehemiah's conflict is rather mild, even if instructive for our model. Another case exists, however, in which the language employed by the groups is much fiercer. The case in question occurred in the early 1980s in the Mexican pilgrimage site and religious colony of Nueva Jerusalén.[109] The colony was founded by Father Nabor and Gabina Romero, the former a Catholic priest (later laicized due to his involvement with the colony) and the latter a voice box through whom it was believed the Virgin Mary spoke. Upon the death of Gabina Romero, a competition for succession developed between two young women in the colony, both of whom claimed to be the rightful heir to Gabina's office.[110] During this competition, one side circulated rumors

---

108. Blenkinsopp, *Ezra-Nehemiah*, 271.

109. Much like the Johannine community, this sect involves a schismatic group experiencing a second schism. The community had, under the leadership of one Father Nabor, earlier separated itself from the Roman Catholic Church. The schism in question involves a further schism within the group after the death of its "voicebox," the intermediary through whom the Virgin Mary spoke. The case is documented by Leatham, "'Shaking Out the Mat," 175–87.

110. Several points are worth noting here. It is first worth pointing out that the case for schism in John's community is strengthened by the fact that these schismatic groups will often resort to violence in enforcing their point of view. Nehemiah will later forcibly drive an opponent from quarters provided him in the Temple complex, the trouble at

about the other that their candidate was a "destroyer of the colony's sanctity. They circulated rumors about her recitations of demonic prayers, alleged sexual liaisons with male monastics, and powers to trick Father Nabor into believing in her charisma."[111] As Leatham notes, the accusations cut right to the heart of the colony's perceived sanctity; as a highly-sectarian apocalyptic group, communication with the Virgin was of utmost importance. To assert that the woman's prayers were actually demonic and therefore deceptive creates a situation in which further devotion to her leadership will result in the group's annihilation along with the rest of the unbelieving world. Similarly, accusations of sexual infidelity feed into this vein of thought and reflect the high premium placed on sexual chastity within the community. We again find here that the rhetoric involved is less an accurate depiction of those against whom it is directed than it is a reflection of the accusing group's own self-perception. We also find the undercutting of legitimacy and dehumanization through associating the voice box with demonic powers, and an attempt to dissociate the voice box from the identity and traditions of the colony by painting her as promiscuous.

A third case comes from a schism that occurred in the mid-1970s within the Presbyterian church in the United States. The driving forces behind this schism, as well as the actual steps taken in effecting the schism, are quite complex and need not be laboriously rehearsed here. The basic facts of the case are that opposing parties arose within the Presbyterian church over the church's position on both social and theological issues such as abortion, the authority of scripture, and the authority of the creeds, the last two being manifested primarily in ecumenical dialogues with others Christian traditions and non-Christian faiths. Though a time-table was initially provided for the resolution of the disagreement, with an accompanying escape clause designed to allow the opposing conservative congregations to separate themselves from the church without forfeiting their local congregational facilities should the resolution not be to their liking, the mounting tensions resulted in the scrapping of the escape clause and

---

Nueva Jerusalén ended in an outburst of violence remembered as La Turba resulting in numerous serious deaths, and 3 John refers to Diotrephes casting "the Brothers" out of the house-church. Secondly, contra Lewis, Wallis's assertion that schism is more likely to occur at the death of the charismatic leader is worth noting. Thirdly, our point regarding rapid group growth is also confirmed inasmuch as Nueva Jerusalén had recently experienced such growth. Not surprisingly, the community split roughly along the lines of new membership versus old.

111. Leatham, "Shaking Out the Mat," 180.

acceleration of the time-table by the liberal forces within the church, thus precipitating the withdrawal of the conservative churches.[112] The language employed by the two sides of this dispute was less vitriolic than what we observed in Nehemiah. The conservative Steering Committee in this dispute released a document in 1972 in which they stated: " . . . we believe that many of the individuals, institutions, boards, and agencies, of the church are apostate, and we see no sign of repentance and revival among them . . . ."[113] The language on the other side was no less harsh. Hillis quotes William P. Thompson, "stated clerk of the UPUSA and well-known liberal," as accusing the conservatives of betraying the trust of their liberal "brethren."[114] Each group's self-perception is easy to detect in their statements. By accusing the liberals of being apostates, the conservatives are implicitly asserting their own orthodoxy and faithfulness to their historic traditions. And not only this, but they also imply the rightness of their relationship to God and the "falling away" of the liberals from faith and right relationship with God. Thompson, on the other hand, by impugning the integrity of the conservatives, implies that he himself has acted with integrity.

We also have the case of Protestant protests against Cathedrals in sixteenth- and seventeenth-century England.[115] This example is particularly significant in that the protesters betray an enormous amount of information quite indirectly and using very few words. Claire Cross quotes *A View of Popishe Abuses*:

> We should be too long to tell your honours of cathedral churches, the dens aforesaid of all loitering lubbers, where master dean, master vicedean, master canons or prebendaries the greater, master petty canons or canons the lesser, master chancellor of the church, master treasurer, otherwise called Judas the pursebearer, the chief chanter, singingmen, special favourers of religion, squeaking choristers, organ players, gospellers, pistellers, pensioners, readers, vergers, etc. live in great idleness and have their abiding. If you would know whence all these came, we can easily answer you, that they came from the pope, as out of the Trojan horse's belly, to the destruction of God's kingdom. The church of God never knew them, neither doth any reformed church in the world know them."[116]

---

112. Hillis, *Can Two Walk Together?*, 31–43.
113. Quoted by Hillis, *Can Two Walk Together?*, 33.
114. Ibid., 7.
115. Cross, "'Dens of Loitering Lubbers,'" 231–38.
116. Ibid., 231.

As Cross points out, the main thrust of the polemic is against the idle and luxuriant lifestyle lived by the cathedral staff and reflects an emphasis on the part of the reformers in having the paid clergy actively involved in preaching.[117] But it also reflects the view that certain members of the staff are involved in misappropriation of funds ("Judas the pursebearer"), and that the cathedral staff members are in secret alliance with the Pope, who has deceptively managed to place these people in their positions with the intent of reclaiming Reformed England for Roman Catholicism. This in turn betrays the religious hostility of the time as well as a heightened sense of paranoia and acceptance of conspiracy theories.[118] The use of brief descriptors and images (Judas, the Trojan Horse) are able to communicate to the reader a great deal of information, but they also reveal the self-perception of the writers: the writers see themselves as reformers (proto-Puritan), true Christians, honest, intending to build up the kingdom of God, and trustworthy.

The language with which one tends to describe one's opponents and their actions in the heat of religious schism also tends to become exaggerated in order to portray one's opponents in the worst possible light, even to the point of dehumanization. Zuckerman quotes Rachel Kantor describing the physical appearance of Lynn Rosefsky and the attitude toward Moishe Kohner, the rabbi of Temple Am Israel, that it betrayed:

> I had always seen Lynn Rosefsky, you know, very pretty woman—had these children I saw here at preschool. I thought: nice lady.... I'm sitting there [in the Temple during service] and she's like—it was the weirdest thing—I mean, her back was like ich! [imitates someone hunched and seething with anger] And it was like: what? And the venom that she put out was just like: huh?[119]

Similarly, Zuckerman records two different accounts given to him of the same incident. Rabbi Kohner took the Temple's Rosh Hashanah service as an opportunity to advocate for gay rights. Though a number of members would confess to Zuckerman their disapproval of Rabbi Kohner's position (see Wallin's remarks above), one member, Camille Vigeland, spoke openly to Rabbi Kohner about her disagreement. The two recollections of

---

117. Ibid., 234–36.

118. These conspiracy theories are not wholly baseless given the ecclesiastical intrigue at the time on the part of both Protestants and Roman Catholics. Their perception, however, is exaggerated beyond the bounds of reality in this tract.

119. Zuckerman, *Strife*, 84.

this event are remarkably different. Yohanna Kohner, Rabbi Kohner's wife, recalls the incident:

> Camille Vigeland rolled her body... she came tumbling down the aisle, and in the process of coming down you could see a whole transformation in her body. By the time she got to Moishe, her nose was twisted, her eyes were screwed-up, and her whole face was held as if she had been hit with a baseball bat. And she bullied him: "You mean to tell me that you're going to educate these homosexual children?!" And he said, "Yes. They are our children ....And Camille said, "Well, I can't have a rabbi who educates with homosexuality!"[120]

Camille Vigeland herself tells a different story:

> ... the rabbi's sister is an outspoken lesbian. Very active. So he kind of jumped on the bandwagon ... so anyway, I met with him privately afterwards ... I was on the executive committee of the board ... and he said, "So what did you think of my High Holiday speech? and I said, "Well, to be honest with you, I don't like you standing up at the pulpit and telling my kids that they can kind of pick and choose among the *mitzvote* (sic).... he went nuts. He told me that, um, I'd become a religious fanatic, and you know, he was embarrassed that he had ever converted me ... and I was becoming just as bad as all those other, you know, Orthodox nutsos, and ... I really—he just went off the deep end.[121]

The differences in the recollections of the event are striking. One would almost think that the same event cannot be in the mind of both informants. Yohanna implies that the altercation took place in the public setting of the Temple sanctuary ("she came tumbling down the aisle") immediately after the sermon while Camille claims that it occurred some time later in a more private setting ("I was on the executive committee of the board"). Yohanna presents Camille as confrontational and bigoted in contrast to the "bullied" rabbi, while Camille presents herself as concerned for the religious upbringing of her children and the rabbi as berating her for her narrow-minded religious conservatism. Additionally, Yohanna describes Camille's physical appearance in a way similar to Rachel Kantor's description of Lynn Rosefsky. Outward physical appearance becomes a canvas upon which the

---

120. Ibid., 112.
121. Ibid., 113.

informant's perception of the inner disposition of the opponent can be graphically represented.

This dehumanizing rhetoric may even extend to the expressed desire that the opponents should die. Julia Wallace, a long-time teacher at Temple Am Israel's Hebrew school, said of Bayt Emmett, "I won't go so far—because I'm a prejudice (*sic*) person—I won't go so far as to say I bless them to do what they are doing. I'd like them to fall through a hole in the earth, frankly. I have no good feelings about those people or what they do."[122] Conversely, one group might also claim that the other wishes their death. According to Judith Malka, Yohanna Kohner, the wife of Rabbi Moishe Kohner, claimed of Bayt Emmett: "You know, they're gonna kill Moishe. And that's when they're going to be happy."[123] Indeed, two months after the schism Kohner resigned Temple Am Israel and moved to the east coast. Less than one month after the move he survived a heart attack, but succumbed to a second heart attack only nine months later. Within a year of the schism, Rabbi Moishe Kohner had died in mid-life. Regarding Kohner's death, Janie Strickstein recalled:

> It was very bitter. It was very bitter . . . when Moishe left and had that heart attack, I mean the bitterness was so bad . . . I had been to a discussion one time . . . where somebody actually stood up and said that the other people—the Bayt Emmett people—were the cause of Moishe's heart attack. Because they had caused so much bitterness.[124]

Judith Malka reported that she had even heard that Abe Shibel had placed a rabbinic curse on Kohner that led to his death, equating the situation with rumors she had heard of a rabbinic curse being placed on Yitzhak Rabin which led to his subsequent assassination.[125] As noted above in the case of Nueva Jerusalén, polemic may lead not simply to the verbal expression of desire for the opponents to die, but to actual physical violence.

A few words ought to be said here in order to tie up some loose ends. Certain of the categories and aspects of schismatic polemics that we have discussed, such as escalation in the intensity of the polemic and impugning one another's morality, are straightforward enough that they need no further comment. Others merit a few final words.

122. Ibid., 197.
123. Ibid., 205.
124. Ibid., 208.
125. Ibid..

Devils and Deviants

The schism in the Presbyterian Church—discussed above—serves as a prime example of the tendency of the two sides in a schism to cast themselves as the true and faithful keepers of the community's religious tradition, though each side may view their faithfulness in markedly different terms.[126] In schisms in which one side may be seen as "traditional" or "conservative" and the other as "progressive" or "liberal," as I will argue is the author's perspective in the case in the Epistles, the traditionalists will argue that they have preserved the letter of the tradition as it has been handed down to them. The constancy and static nature of the tradition is emphasized and preservation of the community's teaching is highly valued. The opponents are cast as going beyond the bounds of what is allowed by the tradition, of being too creative in their theological speculation. They have begun to rely on their own human cleverness rather then the revelation preserved in the community's tradition. Conversely, the progressives will cast the traditionalists as clinging to the letter of the tradition rather than allowing the dynamic spirit of the tradition to lead the community into new truths. The traditionalists then are depicted as being calcified in their adherence to the tradition.

We find in these examples that religious schisms, like many human interactions, tend to elicit harsh rhetoric from the opposing sides. But the rhetoric is not necessarily an accurate description of those against whom the rhetoric is directed. In the case of the Presbyterian schism we have the opportunity to hear each side accusing the other and each side denies the accuracy of the allegations leveled against them. In the cases of Nehemiah and the English cathedrals we have opponents who are voiceless; they are described to us only in the words of the attackers and not in their own words. We would have to imagine that the various staff members of the cathedrals, and Tobiah and Sanballat would have rather different accounts of their activities and motivations. The invective employed by the attackers in these cases is based upon the attackers' own perception of self and reality, and therefore is a more accurate indicator of the attackers' ideology and worldview than it is that of the attacked. Further, the ideology implicitly communicated is of utmost importance to the attackers. The basis for the reformers' attacks on the cathedrals is the need to preach rather than engage in liturgical worship. Nehemiah recounts his conflict with Sanballat and Tobiah as one revolving around his God-given task of rebuilding the walls of Jerusalem. Purity of doctrine and sexual chastity become the

---

126. See Hillis, *Can Two Walk Together?*, 31–43.

flashpoints of the conflict in Nueva Jerusalén, and the inerrancy of scripture as well as the place of the creeds within the life and thought of the church, are the points of controversy in the Presbyterian schism. The point is that the polemic in which the attackers engage communicates what is important to the attackers and not necessarily what is important to those who are attacked.[127]

The opposing parties may also have a tendency to draw upon mythical or traditional language so that short epithets can be used to conjure up a host of negative images, as we saw with the protest against cathedrals. In cases of schism in Jewish or Christian settings, biblical figures are often used in just such a way, with characters such as Judas and Jezebel becoming means of communicating a strongly negative evaluation of the opposing parties. Non-biblical imagery may also be used for the same purpose as long as the image and its negative impact can be easily recognized by the intended audience. Thus we find that non-biblical images like the Trojan horse may be used to indicate nefarious intentions, or calling someone Benedict Arnold to indicate treachery. The specific images used by the author against his or her opponents must be fully explored within their various contexts if the full import of the epithet is to be understood.

Exit Group Formation, the Discourse of Departure, and Defection

A faction within a group may be motivated to schism, and structural and developmental conditions may be conducive to successful schism, but the faction still has to get itself out of the group. How does such a faction manage to leave en masse?

The first step in the actual act of separation from the parent group is the formation of an exit group or groups. These groups continue, in their

---

127. Though we are not examining the theology of the opponents in this work, it ought to be said that the implications of this aspect of the model are quite significant for such an endeavor. In reconstructions of the theology of the opponents, Docetism is always central. This portion of the model calls that into question. What the letters tell us is that the opponents did hold to a Docetic Christology and that this was the greatest point of disagreement *on the part of the Johannine community*. It does not in fact tell us that it was a central doctrine for the opponents, or even that it was the central point of controversy from their perspective. This is not to say that it wasn't, but merely that we must prove that, as well as we are able, rather than simply assuming it because the author asserts as much.

early stages, to operate within the parent group, but will soon enough form the nucleus of a schismatic group that will depart to establish its own movement. They serve as a forum in which disaffected members of the movement can express their increasingly negative evaluation of the larger movement, formulate new sources of legitimation or appropriate established ones, and act upon their feelings of alienation by ultimately separating themselves from the movement. However, these exit groups do not simply appear; their origins can actually be traced back to social groups, cliques, that predate the rise of tensions within the movement.

It is to be expected that sub-groups should form within a larger group or movement, and Stark and Bainbridge see these groups as developing along socio-economic lines within the larger movement.[128] As religious movements develop, they tend toward greater degrees of institutionalization and accommodation to the world which they once rejected. These changes tend to bring greater degrees of material wealth and comfort to the leaders of the movement (see Doherty's description of the orthodox/Hicksite debate within the Society of Friends, above) while many on the lower tiers of the movement are left in more difficult economic straits. These economic disparities give rise to the development of cliques which appeal to the one group or the other, and which mark out social networks and lines of cleavage. Cliques within the same larger group that share similar circumstances and outlooks will reach out to and develop relationships with one another based on shared concerns, while groups with competing agendas will become increasingly distant from one another.

While Stark's and Bainbridge's conclusion that cliques tend to form along socio-economic lines is valid, it cannot be viewed as the only possible explanation for the formation of sub-groups within a movement. E. B. Rochford's study of exit groups confirms the basic premise set forth by Starks and Bainbridge.[129] Rochford briefly describes two schismatic groups within the ISKCON[130] movement and focuses more closely on the second of the two. The Bhaktivedanta Fellowship was composed of a number of business people and entrepreneurs who belonged to ISKCON and, prior to the death of Prabhupada, had joined forces in an attempt to guide the movement to diversify its economic ventures. Prabhupada rebuffed their overtures, but

---

128. Stark and Bainbridge, *Future*, 101–4.

129. Rochford Jr., "Factionalism, Group Defection, and Schism in the Hare Krishna Movement," 162–79.

130. International Society for Krishna CONsciousness.

they redoubled their efforts after his death, only to be rebuffed by the local movement leaders. This final rejection led the leaders of the Fellowship to purchase property for the creation of a separate movement and most in the group defected to this new organization.[131] Similarly, the Conch Club was composed of "householders" (devotees who are married and have children), the majority of whom had worked on the staff of a prominent ISKCON publication. Their initial reason for group formation was, like the Bhaktivedanta Fellowship, promotion of alternative economic strategies for solving the increasing financial difficulties of ISKCON.[132] We shall return to the Conch Club and the processes of exit group formation and discourse momentarily.

Rochford's work does, as we said, confirm the basic premises of Stark's and Bainbridge's proposal that cliques tend to form along socio-economic lines. However, it also introduces a note of complexity into the idea of group formation occurring along socio-economic lines. Stark and Bainbridge, following Niebuhr, argue that socio-economic factors themselves drive both group formation and alienation. In other words, socio-economic disparities dictate with whom one associates, but also fuel a growing sense of alienation on the part of the have-nots. This group tends to view the wealthier movement leadership as in a state of compromise with the outside world, and is therefore viewed as having abandoned or being in the process of abandoning the identity of the movement. The first aspect of Stark's and Bainbridge's proposal seems valid in the case of the two schismatic groups in Rochford's study. The groups seem to be more or less homogeneous in regard to their economic standing and status within the group. However, the economic and social standing of these schismatics is the very opposite of what Stark and Bainbridge expect: they are not at the top echelon of power structures within ISKCON, but they do not seem to have been in the bottom half of ISKCON membership.[133] Further, the concern that drove

---

131. Rochford, "Factionalism, Group Defection, and Schism in the Hare Krishna Movement," 166.

132. Ibid., 166–67.

133. We might classify them as occupants of the "third world" proposed by Johnson, "On Founders and Followers: Some Factors in the Development of New Religious Movements," in *Across the Boundaries of Beief*, 372–73. Johnson argues that new religious movements develop an increasing number of "worlds" occupied by different classes within the movement. In the "two world" stage, the movement is divided between the common followers and the charismatic leader and his/her immediate circle. As the movement develops, however, a third world becomes necessary. This world is occupied by movement members who are charged with the routinization of the movement. "If

the initial formation of each group was not that ISKCON had compromised itself with the world, but that its monolithic economic policy would ultimately be its undoing. A push for economic diversification was what initially brought each of these groups together. As one of Rochford's informants stated the case: "So the [Conch] Club was developed out of people who had similar business interests. In the beginning it was a pretty straight kind of rotary club, very much in connection with ISKCON (*sic*) We were *vaisnava* businessmen interested in helping the movement."[134] However, once the groups formed, emphases began to change. The repudiation of the Conch Club's proposals led to a sense of alienation. This sense of alienation led to a period in which the Club's members began to critically evaluate their own spiritual and psychological development as it related to the larger ISKCON movement and their relationship to conventional society. Of particular concern to the Club members were the movement's strict proscriptions against sexual relations and their sense of limited independence created by "ISKCON's exclusive structure and centralization of power."[135] In other words, Rochford's study has turned that of Stark and Bainbridge on its head: in the case of the Conch Club, socio-economically well-positioned members of ISKCON split off from the larger movement because they felt that the movement had driven too great a wedge between themselves and "normal" society.

We noted above that rapid and significant growth can contribute to tensions within a movement that can eventually result in schism that falls along lines of new versus old membership. Such categorizations are not unexpected nor do they occur suddenly. During the period of growth and prior to the onset of tensions, new members can find the old membership to be a closed social network and so seek out other new members with whom to form relationships. As tensions begin to rise within the movement over issues of power, status, and group identity, social networks begin to crystallize and cleavages become skirmish lines. This process is well illustrated in

---

a religious movement is to survive, a division of labor must develop at the top, which means that the founder becomes dependent on a staff for information and the performance of necessary work, and the staff becomes dependent on the founder for policy directives and for serving as the spiritual center of the movement" (373).

134. Rochford, "Factionalism, Group Defection, and Schism in the Hare Krishna Movement," 167.

135. Ibid., 167–68.

M. Leatham's study of the schism at Nueva Jerusalén, a millenarian sectarian colony in Mexico.[136]

Stark and Bainbridge have made a valuable and valid observation when they note that exit groups have histories that precede the rise of tensions within a group that lead to schism. As with motivation for and propensity to schism, however, we must allow for a greater degree of diversity than does Stark's and Bainbridge's proposal. Other factors, such as ideological orientation, personal relationships (as with Temple Am Israel and quality of relationship to Rabbi Moishe Kohner)[137], and length of membership in the community may all contribute to the formation of cliques within a movement.

Just as we emphasized the *heterogeneity* within the larger group as significant in propensity to schism, so we also must note the importance of *homogeneity* within the clique for the establishing of a successful exit group. The fact that these groups are homogeneous means that events and circumstances that lead to the alienation of one member of the group are very likely to lead to the alienation of most or all of the other members of the group. The existence of homogeneous cliques within the heterogeneous movement sets the stage for the alienation of a large bloc of the movement's members and their subsequent exit from the movement.

In addition to some type of group homogeneity, the presence of a charismatic leader tends to be quite important for successful schism to occur and for the schismatic group to remain together after separation has been effected. G. K. Nelson argues that

---

136. Leatham, "Shaking out the Mat," 177–80. In this case, the death of the "voice-box," or medium for the Virgin Mary, precipitated a succession crisis in which two young women both claimed to be the divinely chosen successor. The colony had experienced recent and substantial growth, and the opposing sides tended to break down along lines of old membership versus new.

137. The exit group in Temple Am Israel was composed of those whose personal relationship with Rabbi Kohner was poor as well as those who had become opposed to the more politically and ideologically liberal positions of Rabbi Kohner. This group had slowly developed relationships with one another over the years as Rabbi Kohner's positions had developed and undergone definition and expansion. The exit group itself began as a Talmud study class, led by one Rabbi Abe Shibel who had consciously chosen not to have any part in Temple Am Israel because of its more liberal orientation. This study class developed into a separate Orthodox Shabbat service, at first held in the home of a group member but later moving within the Temple facilities. See Zuckerman, *Strife*, 138–42, 149–50.

> The charismatic leader focuses the forces for change and brings them to bear upon cracks in the edifice of the existing traditional establishment. In this way, over time, the new movement inspired by the charismatic leader may come to overthrow the existing power structure, whether this be political or religious in form.[138]

Wallis even describes the charismatic leader as "the principal form of authority legitimating schism."[139] This is probably most true in those situations in which the schismatic group must manufacture a new means of legitimation rather than simply appropriate traditional means employed by the parent group. Rochford, in fact, believes that the failure of the Conch Club to achieve any sort of real longevity and long-term cohesion as a group can in part be accounted for by the lack of a charismatic leader among the group's membership.[140] We need not look far in our cases to find a good deal of support for this position. Glendenning was the charismatic figure around whom the Aaronic Order coalesced in leaving LDS,[141] Mama Margarita and Aracadia Arteaga served as the charismatic figures for the two opposing sides in Nueva Jerusalén's schism,[142] and one could make the case that Abe Shibel served this function in the early stages of Bayt Emmett.

Having observed something of the reasons for the formation of these groups, let us move on to the processes by which these groups extricate themselves from the larger movement. The primary activity within the exit group tends to be talking. The group serves as a place where the group members can literally talk themselves out of the larger movement. In better social scientific terminology, the exit group allows its members to engage in a discourse that appropriates means of legitimation by which the group can justify its departure from the parent group. Zuckerman connects this process with V. Turner's "social drama"[143] in which "conflicting groups and personages attempt to assert their own and deplete their opponents' paradigms...."[144] Such a connection adds a further dimension to the discourse

---

138. Nelson, *Cults, New Religions, and Religious Creativity*, 117.

139. Wallis, *Salvation and Protest*, 186.

140. Rochford, "Factionalism, Group Defection, and Schism in the Hare Krishna Movement," 171.

141. Baer, *Utopia*, 146–47.

142. Leatham, "Shaking out the Mat," 179–80. Indeed, had there not been two charismatic figures vying for succession to Gabina Romero's position within the colony, schism may not have occurred.

143. Zuckerman, *Strife*, 151.

144. Turner, *Dramas, Fields, and Metaphors*.

of exit groups: this discourse is meant not only to appropriate legitimation for the exit group, but also to undermine the legitimacy of the parent group.

Temple Am Israel's exit group is a telling example of the working out of this process.[145] The original setting for the exit group, as noted above, was the weekly Talmud class held by Abe Shibel. In the Talmud class, the alienated members of Temple Am Israel began to receive an education in Orthodox Judaism from Shibel. This new-found knowledge then became a basis upon which to criticize Temple Am Israel and Rabbi Kohner's leadership. The group found a new means of legitimation by discovering a different and more ancient way of practicing Judaism. Consequently, this new-found knowledge became a means by which Temple Am Israel could be critiqued, thereby undercutting its legitimacy.

The act of physical separation that follows the exit group's discourse comes by degrees. As already mentioned, some members began to frequent a Talmud study class held by Abe Shibel. After committing to Orthodox Judaism, the group began to hold separate services. These meetings began as once-a-month services held in a private residence.[146] This first instance of separate worship is described by Zuckerman as "the first overt, physical manifestation of the schism."[147] This led to the group meeting at the private residence every Shabbat, but the private residence was becoming constraining for the physical size of the group. A request was made by the group that they be allowed to meet in a back room of the facilities of Temple Am Israel, and this request was granted by the board.[148] A paradox was thereby created in which a faction within Temple Am Israel continued to support the Temple financially and to make use of Temple facilities while holding services completely separate and distinct from and at the same time as that of the other members of the Temple and began to call themselves by a separate name, Bayt Emmett.

At this point, events were set in motion that would increase the level of tension within the community and ultimately lead to the schism proper.[149] Rabbi Kohner's contract came up for renewal and the board, which was fairly evenly divided between those loyal to Kohner and those who

---

145. Zuckerman, *Strife*, 131–38, recounts this early phase.
146. Ibid., 138.
147. Ibid.
148. Ibid., 149–150.
149. Considerations of time and space necessitate and all too brief summary of the detailed treatment provided by Zuckerman, *Strife*, 149–203.

had begun to attend the Bayt Emmett services, began to discuss the matter. Over the objections of the Bayt Emmett faction, the board recommended the extension of a lifetime contract to Rabbi Kohner, prompting the Bayt Emmett faction to circulate a petition opposing the lifetime contract among the members of the Temple.[150] They further held a meeting in the Temple facilities asking for those opposed to the lifetime contract to come and state their grievances openly. The openly hostile attitude of the Bayt Emmett group toward the extension of Rabbi Kohner's contract elicited from those loyal to Kohner a series of verbal attacks that served to entrench each side in their views of one another.[151] The last straw came when Bayt Emmett introduced a *mechitza*[152] into their services. A strongly feminist faction with Temple Am Israel demanded the removal of the mechitza and, when Bayt Emmett refused, circulated a petition among the Temple membership calling for its removal. Rabbi Kohner signed the petition, and with his public rejection of their worship practices, the Bayt Emmett faction fully separated themselves from Temple Am Israel, renting out separate property for their services.

The process by which the Conch Club extricated itself from ISKCON is similar, though less antagonistic.[153] The Conch Club represented a very small group within the much larger ISKCON movement, and, much unlike their counterparts in Bayt Emmett, their defection seems to have passed almost unnoticed by the leadership of ISKCON. At the very least, their defection did not bring about any overt hostility from either side. The Club at first served as a forum in which the householders could reconnect to their lives prior to ISKCON and their initial reasons for joining ISKCON. Such discourse led to expressions of frustration with the way in which

---

150. Ibid., 151. The board's actions in this regard do not appear to have been prompted by Bayt Emmett's opposition to Rabbi Kohner, and therefore only a part of the social drama inasmuch as Bayt Emmett reacted against them.

151. In the first of these attacks, one member of Temple Am Israel confessed to having spread a rumor about a Bayt Emmett couple that he knew, or at least strongly suspected, was untrue. The second attack was the report of a Temple member who attended a few of Shibel's Talmud study classes and claimed that an extremely misogynistic remark was made in the class and that the majority of the Bayt Emmett men present agreed with it. The Bayt Emmett men strongly denied the allegation and claimed that the informant had misheard or misunderstood a conversation in which nothing of the kind was said.

152. A barrier used to separate men and women in more traditional (Orthodox but sometimes Conservative) services in Judaism.

153. Rochford, "Factionalism, Group Defection, and Schism in the Hare Krishna Movement," 167–69.

their personal spiritual lives had developed, or, rather, had not developed. ISKCON's "exclusive structure and centralization of power"[154] had robbed the Club members of "a sense of control over their personal and spiritual lives."[155] Of more importance to the Club members, perhaps, was their increasing dissatisfaction with ISKCON's strict sexual proscriptions, and expressions of dissatisfaction became an important topic of conversation within the Club. In all these discussions, however, the object of dissatisfaction was ISKCON and not Krishna Consciousness itself. Such an approach allowed the Club members to continue practicing their faith together but separated from ISKCON. The legitimacy of Krishna Consciousness was not contested and access to it was available to the members. ISKCON, by hampering rather than promoting their spiritual growth and well-being, had forfeited its legitimacy. Rochford summarizes:

> In sum, the Conch Club served as a 'mediating structure' . . . between ISKCON and the conventional secular society, allowing members to reconstruct their worldview in preparation for exiting. The group prepared its members ideologically for defection by bridging the two familiar, but previously unconnected and seemingly incongruent frames.[156]

The case of William Irvine is also a useful model of the process of talking a group through the act of schism.[157] Irvine was a Scottish evangelist who flourished at the turn of the twentieth century. Through his charismatic persona he attracted a wide following and began to promote radical interpretations of Matthew 10:8-10. He furthered his radical claims by later declaring that only those would be saved who heard the Gospel preached by himself or one of his followers. This second claim was accepted by his followers because it enhanced their own derivative authority. His next claim, however, would not be so accepted by his followers. Irvine claimed that the age of grace would soon come to an end, that Jesus Christ would return to earth in August 1914, and that he had been selected as one of the two witnesses of Revelation. His followers perceived these claims as undercutting rather than strengthening their own derived authority and so alienated

---

154. Rochford, "Factionalism, Group Defection, and Schism in the Hare Krishna Movement," 168.

155. Ibid.

156. Ibid..

157. Johnson, "Founders," 377–78, briefly summarizes the more detailed account provided in Doug Parker and Helen Parker, *The Secret Sect*.

the majority of his followers. Their challenge was to remove Irvine from leadership while preserving Irvine's earlier teachings that legitimated the movement. Johnson's summary of Irvine's ouster is brief enough that it can be reproduced here.

> The workers declared that Irvine "had lost the Lord's anointing" and banned him from all assemblies. But they also had to devise a new source of authority for the movement's very special brand of Christianity. They did this by an ingenious falsification of their own history, in which Irvine's role was obliterated. And armed with this new history and the unity to enforce a ban on Irvine, the workers declared that the founder's name was not to be mentioned within the movement. He was excised from the shared memory of the organization he had founded.[158]

The means by which a schismatic group extricates itself from the parent group usually antedate the very rise of tensions that lead to schism. Heterogeneous movements tend to develop within themselves homogeneous cliques whose members develop strong social networks with one another. These networks sometimes even extend between cliques that have mutual concerns. Cliques may form along a variety of different lines: socioeconomic, length of membership, personal relationships, etc. Their homogeneous nature means that these groups tend to become alienated from the larger movement as a group. Because of their shared concerns, offense and disaffection tend to be widespread when they occur. When alienation occurs, the clique becomes an exit group, a place in which dissatisfaction with the movement can be expressed. These expressions of dissatisfaction lead to the negating of the legitimacy of the parent group and the claiming of legitimacy for the exit group. Such claims lead to a physical separation from the parent group that mirror's the internal alienation that the schismatic group has come to feel toward the parent group. The act of separation itself can occur as a decisive moment, as with the Conch Club, or by degrees, as with Bayt Emmett. Likewise, the act of separation can occur with varying degrees of hostility.

Retrospection

Once the process of schism is complete and association between the two parties ends, retrospection begins. Generally speaking, the schismatic

---

158. Ibid., 378.

group which separates from the parent group tends to dwell on the schism for a lengthy period of time; the painful memory of the split lingers on and continues to be recounted, discussed, and interpreted long after the parent body has moved on to "bigger and better things." This fact complicates any attempt to date a schism by its discussion in a written text or its recounting in an oral text. The fact that a schismatic group discusses a schism does not mean that the event occurred recently.[159] In addition, the schismatic group will continue to interpret its separation from the parent group according to its negative evaluation of the parent group. In other words, the schismatic group will tend to interpret its separation in terms of expulsion or excommunication rather than voluntary exit.

In the case of Temple Am Israel, no official expulsion ever occurred.[160] Though a petition was circulated that opposed the practices of Bayt Emmett within the Temple's facilities, its stated purpose was to prohibit the use of the mechitza. Furthermore, no official action was taken on the petition. It was signed by a limited number of Temple members, including Rabbi Kohner, but it was never submitted to any committee of the Temple or the like. Yet the petition opposing the use of the mechitza was the immediate reason for the separation of Bayt Emmett from Temple Am Israel. Their departure was, apparently, voluntary. No expulsion of any sort, legal or physical, occurred. As Hugh Leon stated it, "It's very clear that they left Temple Am Israel . . . ."[161] But Mike Fish, a member of Bayt Emmett, saw the situation rather differently.

> I felt kicked out. I felt that there was something that could have been done—there could have been a stable equilibrium, remaining in the back . . . but I felt pushed out. I felt pushed out.[162]

In the case of Temple Am Israel and Bayt Emmett, full closure was difficult to achieve. Unlike the Conch Club, which was a small breakaway group

---

159. An illustrative example is found in Giudice, "Persia: Ancient Soul of Iran," 62, who discusses the divisions between Arabs and Iranians. The fact that Arabs conquered the great Persian empire and the oppressions they inflicted on the Perisan people is a lingering source of resentment in Iranian society that had a strong influence on the Iranians' adoption of Shi'ite Islam over against the Sunni Islam of the Arabs. Giudice notes that, "from the vehemence with which they [the Arabs] are still railed against, you would think it happened not 14 centuries ago but last week."

160. Unfortunately, the case of Temple Am Israel is the only study that I have found that includes the participants' recollections of the nature of the separation.

161. Zuckerman, *Strife*, 195.

162. Ibid.

within a relatively large movement situated in one of the largest metropolitan areas in the United States, Bayt Emmett represented a substantial and high-standing group within Temple Am Israel and the small size of Willamette, Oregon virtually ensured that the two sides would continue to run into one another. (Of course, it didn't help that Bayt Emmett chose to rent facilities directly across the street from Temple Am Israel!) Many members of both communities continued to report feelings of intense hostility over a year after the split had occurred. (See above) Kevin Abrams, a member of Temple Am Israel, is representative of the feelings of the other Temple members when he says,

> I have become enjoyably intolerant of Bayt Emmett and what they stand for and what they are doing. And I have no desire to be an integrator . . . I am very upset that they are a half a block away . . . if I never have to deal with those people and their issues, that's fine with me.[163]

Interestingly, the majority of participants in the schism felt not the intense hostility that we have thus far seen, but a deep and profound sense of grief and loss, mingled with a sense of failure in some responsibility to hold the community together.[164] Whatever the reaction, the schism impacted the participants in a profound way. The schism was bitterly fought, the polemics were intense, the issues cut to the core beliefs of the participants and ended decades-long friendships. Even one year down the road, the event continued to hold the attention of the participants and to affect their daily existence in a profound way.

Schism Begets Schism

Schismatic studies have shown that schismatic groups, once they have split from the parent group, tend to continue their schismatic ways.ABDissension and division tends to become a way of life for these groups, Protestantism being a notable example of this phenomenon.

The explanations for this are manifold. As we noted above, Wallis argues that the early stage of a group's existence is a prime time for schism to occur. In the case of a schismatic group, the early stages of the movement's development post-separation can be compared to the early stages of a new

---

163. Ibid., 197.
164. Ibid., 197–203.

religious movement. The challenges that face a new religious movement during this period are comparable to those that a schismatic group will face: the boundaries of the new leader's authority have not been fully tested, the group's means of legitimation may not be fully in place, and authority structures have not been solidified. All of these factors mean that the schismatic group may itself experience a second schism shortly after separating itself from the parent group. Additionally, the schismatic group may adopt means of legitimacy that rank them high on Wallis's scale of propensity to schism. The schismatic group may have inherited these means of legitimacy from their parent group or they may have manufactured them. A third possibility is that the charismatic leadership necessary for the group to maintain cohesion post-schism is either absent or poorly executed. We noted an example of this in the case of the Conch Club. In this case, the Club consciously shunned charismatic leadership and adopted a highly democratic form of self-governance. This choice resulted in a lack of group cohesion and an inability to draw in new membership. As a consequence, the group fragmented and dissolved within a year of its establishment. While these three possibilities do not exhaust the varying causes for continuing schism within a group, they do serve as some of the more common reasons for this happening and illustrate the point well.

Summary

Before proceeding to the application of the model to the texts in question, let us take a moment to summarize briefly what we have said thus far. In order for a schism to occur, some smaller unit within the larger group must be motivated to separate itself. Though motivation was at one time viewed strictly in socio-economic terms, a new perspective has arisen within schismatic studies that sees a variety of motivations behind schisms. Ambition, a desire for status, can prompt schism, as can a sense of alienation from the larger group. Additionally, ideological considerations that do not directly arise from socio-economic factors can motivate a group to separate itself.

The likelihood that schism will occur within a given group is impacted by the means of legitimation appropriated by the larger group and by whether smaller groups within it have access to those means. Larger groups may understand themselves as uniquely legitimate or pluralistically legitimate. Uniquely legitimate groups define their beliefs sharply, with a strong emphasis on doctrinal specificity and a high premium placed on adherence to the group's doctrine. Pluralistically legitimate groups define their beliefs less sharply and therefore tolerate a greater degree of deviation within the ranks than do uniquely legitimate groups, leading to a lower incidence of schism.

From a structural standpoint, groups with a more centralized authority structure are less prone to schism as the means of legitimation are beyond the reach of the exit groups that must appropriate them in order to be successful in separating from the larger group. Less centralized groups are more likely to experience schism because access to legitimacy is more open. However, more centralized groups may also lack the mechanisms necessary for dealing with internal conflict, in which case rising tensions within the group may still result in schism, and possibly through a more acrimonious and therefore painful process because of the difficulty in appropriating means of legitimacy.

The means of legitimation appropriated by the larger group fall generally within two categories: charismatic and ideological. Charismatic legitimation centers on an individual who forms the group's identity through the force of his own personality. Within these groups, schism is low because legitimacy lies within a single person. Tensions tend to run high in these groups, with differing factions competing for the favor of the charismatic leader, but those tensions are defused through the peace-making actions of the charismatic leader, who enhances his own status by mediating truces between rival factions. Ideological groups tend to have a higher propensity toward schism because the intellectual basis for the group can be more easily appropriated by exit groups.

Finally, the more means of legitimation are available to exit groups, the higher the likelihood that they will be able to appropriate some means of legitimacy and successfully leave the parent group. Conversely, the fewer the legitimating institutions, the more difficult they are to appropriate, and therefore the likelihood that schism occurs decreases.

Along with institutional considerations, there are certain developmental stages within a group that make schism more likely. At the formation of the group, institutional structures are lacking, means of legitimacy are less clearly defined, and larger numbers of groups have access to those means, making schism more easily attained. At times of rapid growth, a sense of alienation from the group can be heightened, thus also making schism more likely. Finally, the death of the charismatic leader can often lead to schism as various new or existing tensions within the group come to a head.

The process by which an exit group forms and removes itself from the parent group is referred to as the "schismatic dance." This process begins with clique formation—the formation of a group or groups whose members have similar concerns and goals. These groups, in order to separate themselves successfully, must appropriate some means of legitimation, which is generally accomplished by engaging in polemics against the parent group. These polemics involve the use of exaggeration, symbolic language, accusations of violence and sexual deviance, accusations of deviance from the community's traditions and/or ideals, and dehumanizing language. After schism has been successfully achieved, the exit group—and sometimes the parent group—will engage in a continued period of polemical retrospection. This activity allows the exit group to solidify its legitimacy and justify its decision to leave the parent group. If the parent group engages in retrospection, it is generally because the exit group was large enough and the schism painful enough to wound the parent group upon its departure.

III

Presuppositions Moving Forward

HAVING SET UP AND summarized our model, let us make a few preliminary observations about the state of Johannine studies before quickly moving to apply our model to the text of 1 and 2 John.

The Epistles and the Gospel

The relationship between Gospel and Epistles is one that has received and continues to receive its fair share of attention, and the question of literary dependency and chronological ordering of these texts are closely related topics within the discussion. That the Gospel and Epistles are closely related to one another is not seriously disputed, and articulating a chronology of the Johannine literature allows us to use the earlier texts to understand the development and thought of the later texts. Though a lengthy rehearsal of the scholarship on this topic is not advisable here, I will briefly present some of the major opinions on this matter and indicate my own position.

Fairly typical of the position that the Letters were written prior to the Gospel is Strecker.[1] Strecker first argues that 2 and 3 John are written by the same author, as indicated by the common designation ὁ πρεσβύτερος for the sender, and that "the situation presupposed by both letters" is the same.[2] 2 John, Strecker argues, was written prior to 3 John. Because of the

---

1. Strecker, *Letters*, xl. This position, with some variation, seems to be championed most often by German scholarship. See also Schnelle, *New Testament Writings*, 439; and Vogler, *Die Briefe des Johannes*, 3–6. However, this position has also found support in Britain and the United States. See Grayston, *Epistles*, 7–12; Segovia, "The Theology and Provenance of John 15:1-17," 11–128; and Talbert, *Reading John*, 4, who argue that the composition of the Epistles and the Gospel occurred at about the same time or that the Epistles were written prior to the Gospel.

2. Strecker, *Letters*, xl.

Presuppositions Moving Forward

lack of the title ὁ πρεσβύτερος, form-critical differences, and differences in theology and church discipline, Strecker argues that 1 John was written by a different author than that of 2 and 3 John, and reflects a later phase in the development of the community. The Gospel reflects a still later phase in the community's history and is in part written to help the community deal with the lingering effects of the struggles that are reflected in the Letters.

The reverse of this argument is that the Gospel precedes the Epistles and that there is insufficient evidence to reject the canonical order of the Epistles. Brown has served as the main proponent of this position.[3] He notes wide agreement that 2 and 3 John were written at about the same, but argues that there is not enough evidence to determine which might have actually been written first. In the case of 1 John, the same general situation seems to be addressed as in 2 John, though 2 John seems to have been written to a congregation at a geographical distance from the author of 1 John and the secessionists and their teachings have not yet made their way into this congregation. The end result of this analysis, Brown concludes, is that "it is perfectly possible ... that the three Johannine Epistles were composed about the same time and dealt with ramifications of the same problem throughout the Johannine churches."[4] Regarding the relationship of the Epistles to the Gospel, Brown argues that the connection between the two is more than the mere sharing of ideas. Rather, it represents a situation in which the secessionists have exaggerated the claims of the Gospel and the epistolary author is attempting to correct their misinterpretation.[5] The result is that Brown regards the Gospel as written first with the Epistles following some time later and written closely together. Though the ordering of the Epistles cannot be determined with certainty, Brown sees no reason to reject the canonical order.

A third option attempts to mediate between these two positions and has been promoted most notably by Hengel.[6] Hengel proposes a reconstruction of the writing of these texts in which the Gospel developed through the oral teaching of John the Elder over a very long period of time. Toward the end of this process the Elder began to commit his oral teachings to writing

---

3. Brown, *Epistles*, 30–35. See also Painter, *1, 2, and 3*, 74; and Smalley, *1, 2, 3, Revised*, xx. For a modification of this proposal, see Thomas, *1 John, 2 John, 3 John*, 12, who maintains the priority of the Gospel, but reverses the canonical order of the Epistles.

4. Brown, *Epistles*, 32.

5. Ibid., 35.

6. Hengel, *Question*, 24–73.

in a collection of notes and one or more outlines for the written Gospel. The oral teaching was disseminated throughout the Johannine school and certain Gentile Christians in the school began to misinterpret the oral teaching to such a degree that John the Elder felt it necessary to address the issue through three epistles. After the death of the Elder, his disciples used the outline(s) he had written and assembled his written notes, with minimal editing, into the Gospel. Hengel's proposal combines elements of both of the aforementioned proposals. Like the first proposal, Hengel argues that the actual writing of the Gospel was subsequent to the Epistles. Like the second proposal, however, he also argues that the ideas and basic narrative of the Gospel were already in place and their misinterpretation by the secessionists led to the writing of the Epistles.

I find Hengel's proposal to be compelling, especially regarding the nature of the composition of the Gospel. The common point between Hengel and Brown, that the Epistles were written as a response to the misinterpretation of the ideas found in the Gospel, seems to me more persuasive than the alternative represented by Strecker.[7] Whether the Gospel existed as a written or oral text, I will assume that it was composed and disseminated in the Johannine community prior to the Epistles. Regarding the sequencing of the Epistles, I must also concur with Brown. Reconstructions that posit a highly specific ordering for the Epistles are unpersuasive and place too great a burden on the evidence. The evidence would suggest instead that the Epistles were composed so near to one another that sequencing them seems to be virtually unnecessary.

Schism in the Gospel?

If the Johannine Epistles are regarded as arising *within* the context of schism, many interpreters of John's Gospel see it as emerging *out of* a schism. John's references to ἀποσυνάγωγος have led to a vigorous discussion of the possibility that the Johannine community was at one point in its past embedded within the broader non-Christian Jewish community but was then violently expelled because its theology had begun to diverge too sharply

---

7. I do not find Strecker's form-critical argument compelling and believe that his case for theological differences between 1 John on the one hand and 2 and 3 John on the other is overstated. I do find persuasive, however, Brown's arguments that 1 and 2 John are too similar in theology, vocabulary, and style to have been written by two different authors. Subjective though it is, I cannot shake the impression that the Epistles, especially 1 John, seem to have the Gospel in their background rather than vice versa.

from that of non-Christian Jews. The questions of an earlier separation from the synagogue and the reasons that might have occurred are worth our consideration prior to examining the schism in the letters as such a past event would increase the propensity to schism within the Johannine community. Additionally, understanding the reasons the Johannine community separated from the non-Christian Jewish community may in fact help us to understand the ideological identity of the Johannine community and thus better understand the reasons for the schism evident in the Epistles. As we shall see, the Gospel's use of ἀποσυνάγωγος language is not a guarantee that the Johannine community was forcibly expelled from the synagogue, and that the likely reason for the separation between Johannine community and synagogue was the increasingly high Christology of the former, which became incompatible with the theology of the latter.

On three occasions the Gospel of John makes use of the term ἀποσυνάγωγος: 9:22; 12:42; and 16:2. These three are the only uses of this term in the whole of the Greek Bible (LXX and NT). Since at least the time of Westcott, this term has been understood to mean some sort of official exclusion from the synagogue, though Westcott does not specify the nature of this exclusion.[8] Bernard ventures more specificity by arguing that the expulsion envisioned in John's Gospel is of a briefer period, probably only a month.[9] Barrett carries the historical reconstruction of the use of this term even further by contradicting Bernard and asserting that the use of ἀποσυνάγωγος would have referred to a permanent exclusion from the synagogue.[10] He further argues that the *Birkath ha-minim*, the Twelfth Benediction or Benediction for the Heretics, was the means by which this expulsion was achieved and that some Jewish Christians who had experienced this expulsion would have been among John's readers.

J. Louis Martyn's work on the subject of expulsion in *History and Theology in the Fourth Gospel* has come to be seen as a watershed in Johannine studies, with A. Reinhartz going so far as to compare the impact of Martyn's work on the Johannine scholarship of the second half of the twentieth century to that of Bultmann's in the first half.[11] In *History and Theology*, Martyn essentially reiterates the positions taken by Barrett regarding the nature of the expulsion and the means by which expulsion occurred. His

---

8. Westcott, *The Gospel According to St. John*, 2:37–38.
9. Bernard, *Gospel According to St. John*, 2:334.
10. Barrett, *The Gospel According to St. John*, 299–300.
11. Reinhartz, "Reading History in the Fourth Gospel," 191.

innovation is to cast the stories mentioning ἀποσυνάγωγος as "two-level dramas" in which the Gospel's tales of expulsion directly reflect the experiences of the Johannine community itself. The story is both a witness to the historical ministry of Jesus Christ and "a witness to Jesus' powerful presence in actual events experienced by the Johannine church."[12] Such a reading leads Martyn to reconstruct the Johannine community's history as beginning within the synagogue as a messianic group that experienced a good amount of success with its preaching. As the group's Christology developed, however, it aroused the suspicions of synagogue leaders, who introduced a re-worded form of the *Birkath ha-Minim* in order to ferret out these Jewish Christians. This resulted in the permanent expulsion from the synagogue of these Jewish Christians and even the martyrdom of some.[13]

It would be difficult to overstate the impact that Martyn's proposal has had on Johannine studies. Indeed, his basic assertion, that the Johannine Christians experienced a forcible and intentional expulsion from the synagogue, has attained nearly axiomatic status. Perhaps the most prominent scholar to adopt the basic framework proposed by Martyn was Brown, who assimilated Martyn's proposal into his own reconstruction of the history of the Johannine community with only minor alterations,[14] and acceptance of Martyn's two-level reading cuts across the ideological/theological spectrum of Johannine interpreters.[15]

Acceptance of Martyn's proposal has not been universal, however. Some interpreters have expressed a degree of reluctance to accept Martyn's reading, labeling it inconclusive at best and too speculative at worst.[16] The primary point of critique is Martyn's assertion that the *Birkhat ha-Minim* served as the tool by which synagogue leaders could discover Christians in their midst,[17] and Martyn has recently evaluated that aspect of his

---

12. Martyn, *History and Theology*, 40.

13. Ibid., 147–57.

14. Brown, *Community of the Beloved Disciple*, 22. Brown maintained this position throughout the remainder of his career. See *An Introduction to the Gospel of John*, 74–78.

15. Martyn's Proposal is accepted in some form by scholars as diverse as Tenney, *John: The Gospel of Belief*, 159; Keener, *Gospel*, 1:194–98; Moloney, *Gospel*, 294, 298; Smith, *Johannine Christianity*, 209–10; Lincoln, *Gospel*, 284; and O'Day, "The Gospel of John," 657.

16. Carson, *The Gospel according to John*, 369–72; Morris, *The Gospel according to John*, 434–35, esp. n36.

17. See especially Katz, "Issues in the Separation of Judaism and Christianity after 70 C.E.: A Reconsideration ," 43–76; Kimmelman, "*Birkat Haminim* and the Lack of

reconstruction as "somewhat uncertain."[18] A recent critic of Martyn's is Reinhartz, who goes beyond criticisms of Martyn's understanding of the use of the *Birkhat ha-Minim* and argues against some of his foundational methodological approaches.

Reinhartz argues that if the two-level reading of John's Gospel is valid it should be applicable beyond those passages mentioning ἀποσυνάγωγος,[19] and so sets out to test the validity of the two-level reading on other stories mentioning οἱ Ἰουδαῖοι in John's Gospel.[20] Reinhartz notes that Mary and Martha are comforted by οἱ Ἰουδαῖοι in 11:19, and in 12:11, many Jews come to believe in Jesus because of the resuscitation of Lazarus and yet suffer no repercussions. From this comparison of the results of a two-level reading of three different stories in John's Gospel, Reinhartz argues that she has uncovered three historical models for the Johannine community's relationship with the synagogue: (1) forcible expulsion of the Johannine Christians, (2) cooperation between Johannine Christians and traditional synagogue members, and (3) voluntary exit of the Johannine Christians. Reinhartz concludes that the difficulties of the two level reading make this approach "difficult to maintain,"[21] instead concluding that the Gospel presents itself as "an authoritative presentation of Jesus"[22] and that the Gospel should be read as presenting the historical time of Jesus, whether the presentation is historically accurate or not.[23]

Reinhartz's critique has garnered the approval of Carter,[24] who has also recently offered his own explanation for the occurrences of ἀποσυνάγωγος.

Evidence for an Anti-Christian Jewish Prayer in Late Antiquity," 226–44, 391–403; Boyarin, *Border Lines*; and Van der Horst, "The *Birat Ha-Minim* in recent Research," 367–68.

18. Martyn, "The Johannine Community Among Jewish and Other Early Christian Communities," 187.

19. Of the several publications in which Reinhartz has made this argument, she most clearly articulates her reasoning in "The Johannine Community and Its Jewish Neighbors: A Reappraisal," 117–18, where she argues, "If this is the case [that expulsion from the synagogue represents the central historical experience of the Johannine community], than it is reasonable to expect that a two-level reading of the Gospel as a whole will paint a picture that supports, or at least is consistent with, the expulsion theory."

20. Reinhartz, *Befriending the Beloved Disciple*, 40–41.

21. Ibid., 51.

22. Ibid.

23. Ibid., 50.

24. See Carter, *John: Storyteller, Interpreter, Evangelist*, 166–67, where he notes Reinhartz's discovery of three contradictory model based on the two-level reading, concluding that there are a number of problems involved in maintaining the historical

Like Reinhartz, Carter catalogues the difficulties in accepting Martyn's hypothesis, much of which revolves around the critique of Martyn's reconstruction of the formulation and purpose of the *Birkhat ha-Minim*.[25] Based on this critique, Carter concludes that "the case for the synagogue's bitter expulsion of the Jesus believers has not been made."[26] His proposed alternative is that the instances of ἀποσυνάγωγος in John's Gospel are performative rather than reflective.[27] The author(s) of the Gospel of John does not include these passages because they reflect the experience of an embattled sectarian group suffering persecution from its Jewish parent group because of its lofty Christology. On the contrary, the Johannine Christians are, in the view of the author(s), much too comfortable in their relationship with the synagogue and with the wider Roman imperial world. The Gospel is intended to create conflict and distance between the Johannine Christians and these two larger contexts. In other words, the references to ἀποσυνάγωγος do not present the world as it *is* but as the author(s) believes it *ought* to be.

The critique of Martyn has not gone unnoticed in the larger field of Johannine studies and is garnering increasing support. However, the critique itself is not unproblematic. Reinhartz's strong focus on the use of Ἰουδαῖοι seems to shift the emphasis away from the central focus of Martyn's study, the use of ἀποσυνάγωγος. Reinhartz is aware of the centrality of the ἀποσυνάγωγος passages to Martyn's study, but argues that the two-level drama cannot be restricted to them if this is indeed a valid reading strategy.[28] However, the remarkably flexible way in which John uses Ἰουδαῖος (even if it often, or even usually, has a highly negative value[29]) ought to

---

reconstructions of Martyn and Brown.

25. Carter, *John and Empire*, 24–25.
26. Ibid., 26.
27. Ibid.
28. Reinhartz, "Reading History in the Fourth Gospel," 193.
29. Johnson, "'Salvation is from the Jews,'" 83–100, notes that the scholarly consensus regarding John's view of Jews and Judaism is often exaggerated toward the negative. He is correct in noting that John's attitude toward Judaism is "not one of outright rejection; instead it is both acceptance and rejection" (98). John imports Judaic categories into the formulation of his Christology, but these categories are reframed in light of Christ. They both inform and are informed by John's developing Christology. This implies some degree of positive evaluation of the Jewish background from which John emerged while at the same time maintaining that John has reinterpreted his Jewish matrix. Still, it would seem that when John speaks specifically of οἱ Ἰουδαῖοι these characters are portrayed as hostile opponents.

caution us against connecting the idea of expulsion so closely to "the Jews" that every use of the latter must also reflect the former. Indeed, the flexibility of Johannine language in general ought to serve as a caution against such hard and fast conclusions. In addition, the Johannine community is largely regarded as having a background in Palestinian Judaism,[30] yet it is able to make strong distinctions between itself and Judaism. Discounting a schism from the synagogue earlier in the community's history makes explaining this development not impossible but certainly more complicated.[31] On the other hand, acceptance of the schism makes this development more understandable. Reinhartz and others have raised important questions about Martyn's methodological approach and subsequent conclusions and have rightly brought into question Martyn's assertion that the separation of the Johannine community from the synagogue is the controlling event for understanding the community and its theology. In the final analysis, however, schism from the synagogue makes the best sense of the evidence.

However, Martyn's precise (perhaps overly precise) reconstruction of the events surrounding the schism may not be tenable. Two points made by Martyn are worth considering: (1) that the Johannine Christians were expelled[32] from the synagogue, and (2) that the expulsion and its aftermath were violent, even to the point that some Johannine Christians were killed. The example of Temple Am Israel noted above is quite a good example of how the historical circumstances surrounding a schism can be remembered very differently by the two parties involved.[33] The Bayt Emmett group consistently saw themselves as having been removed or forced out of Temple Am Israel. While such a recollection has some basis in fact, it cannot be said that it is an entirely accurate assessment of events. The action that drove Bayt Emmett to leave Temple Am Israel was the circulation of a petition barring the use of a *mechitza* on the premises of Temple Am Israel and the signing of that petition by the congregation's rabbi, Moishe Kohner.

---

30. See Keener, *John*, 1:143.

31. For instance, Hakola, *Identity Matters*, 215–16, 218, argues against a schismatic reading of John's Gospel, but then admits that some sort of "break" (though not as complete a break as the Gospel's author would have liked) must have occurred between the Johannine community and Judaism.

32. We should keep in mind that forcible expulsion is not a requisite for schism, though it may often occur in the schismatic process. Instead, what defines schism is that the two sides separate themselves from one another, which may in fact happen by mutual consent as well as by force.

33. See Zuckerman, *Strife*, 195.

So action was taken that struck at a prominent symbol of Bayt Emmett's newfound Jewish Orthodoxy. However, the petition did not say that Bayt Emmett could not worship in Temple Am Israel facilities, only that they could not use a *mechitza* in doing so. Further, the petition was never acted upon by the board or the congregation. In fact, it is not clear that the anti-*mechitza* group would have been successful in their endeavor since many of the congregants later expressed permissive attitudes toward Bayt Emmett's practices. So while the negativity expressed by some in Temple Am Israel toward Bayt Emmett's practices caused Bayt Emmett to feel extremely unwelcome in and ultimately forced out of Temple Am Israel, there was never any official action expelling them from the congregation.

Later recollections of negatively charged personal encounters between members of the two sides in the Temple Am Israel schism also tended to diverge sharply. Opposing members tended to describe one another in almost impossible, and at least improbable, physical postures and actions. Verbal exchanges were described in quite different terms depending upon which side of the debate one took. Yohanna Kohner described her husband as verbally assaulted, bullied, by Camille Vigeland, while Vigeland herself described Rabbi Kohner's response to her as overly hostile and disproportionate to her remarks. Each side cited the other as the instigator of the conversation. The rhetoric even reached the point that members of Temple Am Israel blamed the Bayt Emmett group for Moishe Kohner's subsequent death by heart attack. This blame ranged from assertions that the strain of the schism led to his heart attack to the suggestion that Bayt Emmett placed a rabbinic curse upon Kohner that led to his death. Either way, Moishe Kohner's terminal cardiac arrest on the Atlantic coast was blamed on a small enclave of Orthodox Jews in the Pacific Northwest.

The implications for understanding the Johannine community and its history are obvious. It can be maintained that a schism occurred in the Johannine community while also entertaining the possibility that the schism was not effected through an official and violent expulsion. The Johannine Christians may very well have felt "kicked out." They may very well have seen the synagogue leaders as conspiring against them. They may very well have felt that later deaths in their membership could somehow be attributed to "the Jews." The reality, however, is that they may simply have left the synagogue voluntarily. My assumption moving forward, then, is that the Johannine community became separated from its Jewish parent group over the issue of the former's Christology. Whether they were violently expelled or left voluntarily cannot be said with any certainty.

Christological controversy would still seem to be the catalyst for this separation. It remains to be seen if the Johannine community's Christology had reached the high level found in the Gospel prior to the schism, or if the schism contributed to an increasingly higher Christological formulation. L. Hurtado allows that "disputation can cause participants to reflect further on their convictions, leading to intensification, refinements, and noticeable developments in the way convictions are expressed and even in their substance."[34] However, Hurtado argues that there is insufficient diachronic evidence to safely reconstruct such Christological developments and further argues that there is evidence for a high, possibly even equally high, Christology among Christians prior to the writing of the Gospel, thereby arguing that a lower Christology need not be assumed for the early period of the community's history.[35] However, Hurtado still allows that the presentation of the community's Christology in the Gospel is reflective of strong controversy with the synagogue. On the other hand, a scenario might also be imagined in which a high Christology became higher as a result of conflict with non-Christian Jews. In a highly charged, schismatic scenario, the two sides may very well have taken increasingly extreme positions as they countered one another. Johannine assertions of the divinity of Jesus would have been met with strong denials of this, resulting in stronger proclamations of Jesus' divinity that elicited more strenuous protestations to the contrary, and so on. In other words, given the back-and-forth process that the polemics of schism often take, an already high Christology might have become even more so as the Johannine community worked through the process of separating itself from its Jewish parent group.[36] Whether it is argued that the community's Christology was low early on and became increasingly higher as the schism proceeded, or that the community's Christology had reached full bloom by the time of the schism, Christology remains at the center of the controversy with the synagogue

---

34. Hurtado, *Lord Jesus Christ*, 405.

35. Ibid., 405–7.

36. Ashton, *Understanding the Fourth Gospel*, 281, makes a similar argument, asserting that the polemics of the Gospel remind one "of those fierce family rows whose surprising virulence is intelligible only if they are heard against the background of a long history of mutual incomprehension and mistrust." Such an understanding, of course, circumscribes the need for positing an influx of Samaritan converts in order to account for the heightening of John's Christology, as does Brown, *Community*, 43–47.

and so will figure prominently in my understanding of the community's sense of legitimacy.

The Johannine Literature and the Book of Revelation

The question of the relationship of Revelation to the Gospel of John and the Epistles has a long and storied history too long to fully rehearse here.[37] Indeed, better scholars than I have concluded that little if anything can be said positively about the relationship, and other, perhaps even wiser, scholars have intentionally eschewed the question altogether. Nevertheless, it will become evident that Revelation may have something to contribute to our understanding of the Johannine community as uniquely legitimate, if in fact some connection between the two can be established.

In modern times, as in ancient, the question of this relationship tends to revolve around authorship: if the author of Revelation was responsible for at least one of the other Johannine texts, its connection to the Johannine community would be unquestionable; conversely, any assertion that Revelation was composed by an author different from that of the Gospel or Epistles would immediately complicate the question. The latter position is taken by the majority of scholars today, though the former is not without its adherents.[38]

The argument against common authorship tends to fall along linguistic and theological lines. Commentators often note that Dionysisus of Alexandria first observed the linguistic differences between Revelation and

---

37. See particularly Epiphanius, *Haer.* 51.33; and Eusebius, *Hist. Eccl.* 2.28.1–2, for early disputes over the apostolic authorship of Revelation. We ought also to note here that the discussion of the relationship of Revelation to the Johannine community has been primarily carried out as a discussion of the relationship of Revelation to the Gospel of John. Since it is largely accepted by contemporary scholarship that one community, if not one hand, produced both the Gospel and the Epistles, I will simply make use of the present scholarly discussion of Revelation and the Gospel of John rather than blazing new trails with a comparison of Revelation to the Epistles.

38. The argument that both Revelation and another Johannine writing come from the same hand is generally associated with arguments for the apostolic authorship of Revelation. Among those who continue to make such an affirmation are Mounce, *The Book of Revelation*, 25–31; and especially Smalley, *Thunder and Love*, 35–40; and Smalley, *The Revelation to John*, 2–3. Beale, *The Book of Revelation*, 34–36; Boxall, *The Revelation of Saint John*, 5–7; Guthrie, *Introduction to the New Testament*, 932–48; Osborne, *Revelation*, 2–6; and Swete, *The Apocalypse of St. John*, clxxxv, are hesitant to ascribe authorship to John son of Zebedee, but are more hesitant to rule out this possibility.

the Gospel of John,[39] and the linguistic argument is often seen as of primary importance in arguing that the Gospel and Revelation could not have been authored by the same person.[40] In addition, a number of differences between the theology of the Gospel of John and Revelation have been noted. Probably of greatest significance are the divergent eschatological outlooks of the two texts, Revelation being seen as having a strongly futurist eschatology and Gospel of John as having a strongly realized eschatology.

In spite of these differences, there are also points of correspondence between the Gospel of John and the Epistles on the one hand, and Revelation on the other. Revelation and the Gospel of John are the only New Testament documents that refer to Jesus as λόγος and Witherington notes a number of similarities in diction.[41] V. S. Poythress argues that Rev. 1:1-8 and 1:17b-3:22 are closest in genre to the Gospel and Epistles, and evidence a close literary relationship with one another based upon their use of conjunctions.[42] Similarly, Whale has argued that R. H. Charles's assessment of the lexical differences between the Gospel of John and Revelation are overstated, particularly with regard to ἀρνίον, καλέω, ἔθνος, κόσμος, ἕως, and μαρτυρέω.[43] Osborne notes ἐκκεντέω to translate Zech 12:10, which is absent in LXX, as well as several other terms used only in John's Gospel and Revelation.[44] In addition, 1 John and Revelation are the only two books of the New Testament to use the verb σφάζω, "to slaughter," with 1 John 3:12 employing it graphically to describe the assault of Abel by Cain as an illustration of the actions of the schismatics, and Revelation using it at 5:6, 9, and 12; 6:4, and 9; 13:3 and 8; and 18:24 to describe both the Lamb and the martyred witnesses who stand beneath the altar. Boxall makes the point most pertinent to my own argument when pointing out that both John's Gospel and Revelation are associated with the city of Ephesus from a very early date.[45] What implications should be drawn from these data for understanding the relationship of Revelation to the Johannine community?

---

39. Witherington III, *Revelation*, 2.

40. Ibid., 2–3; see also Aune, *Revelation*, 1:clx–ccxi, for an exhaustive discussion of the peculiarities of Revelation's language.

41. Ibid., 3.

42. "Johannine Authorship and the Use of Intersentence Conjunctions in the Book of Revelation," 329–36.

43. "The Lamb of John," 289–95.

44. Osborne, *Revelation*, 5.

45. Boxall, *The Revelation of Saint John*, 7. Note, however, that Boxall does not posit common authorship and maintains an agnosticism about the identity of John the

While the argument that John the Revelator is also the author of John's Gospel and Epistle is too positive an assessment of the evidence, the denial of any sort of relationship between the two texts may go to the other extreme. It would seem that we might be on more firm footing if we were to argue that all five texts have their origins in the Johannine community in western Asia Minor, though they may not all have been authored by the same person. Given the early and consistent witness that all the texts arose within the same geographical locale, a shared apocalyptic worldview, and similar use of less commonly occurring terminology, this seems a tenable position. Though I would not accept without qualification that this author is a good representative of the entirety of Johannine theology,[46] I believe that that he does share and enhance our knowledge of the Johannine community's evaluation of Greco-Roman religion. For this reason, I will make limited use of Revelation as I attempt to reconstruct the Johannine community's view of itself as a uniquely legitimate group.

The Question of 3 John

I noted early on this study the fact that modern scholarship tends to view 3 John as addressing a situation different than that addressed in 1 and 2 John. Smalley sums up this perspective nicely when he states, "By the time 3 John was written, the unity of the Johannine circle appears to have been considerably threatened from an organizational, as well as doctrinal, point of view."[47] The understanding of the exact nature of this organizational difficulty has changed over the years, however. For many years, the dominant paradigm was that of Harnack, who argued that Diotrephes was a monarchical bishop who was leading his local congregation toward an organizational structure more akin to that being used in the emerging catholic church.

Revelator. Similarly Blount, *Revelation*, 6, who closely identifies Revelation with western Asia Minor.

46. That is, if we are even able to speak of a Johannine theology in the sense of a theological system uniformly accepted by all members, or at least the leading members, of the community. It would seem more likely to me that we should expect to see some degree of variation in theology within the Johannine community.

47. Smalley, *1, 2, 3 John*, xxviii. A few notable exceptions do exist. Bauer, *Orthodoxy and Heresy in Earliest Christianity*, 61–146, argues that Diotrephes is a heretic who has been excommunicated by the Elder, while Käsemann, "Ketzer und Zeuge: Zum johanneischen Verfasserproblem," 292–311, turns this proposition on its head, arguing that Diotrephes has excommunicated the elder for heresy.

Since Harnack's proposal, A. Malherbe has argued that the primary issue in dispute is not that of organization per se, but hospitality and Diotrephes' refusal to extend it to the Elder's emissaries.[48] In Malherbe's model, the Elder had sent emissaries who had been rejected by Diotrephes, who was the householder hosting the local Johannine congregation. This rejection of the Elder's emissaries was construed by the Elder as a rejection of himself, but the issue was personal rather than doctrinal or organizational. Whatever the particulars, the common view of the situation behind 3 John leads most scholars to exclude it from any discussion of the schism in 1 and 2 John since this issue was doctrinal and ethical. However, this may be a misreading of the evidence.

In the social scientific study of sects and new religious movements, it has been observed that doctrinal and organizational control within the movement often go hand in hand and occur to the same degree. As group leadership more precisely defines the group's belief system, there is a corresponding centralization of power. With this in mind, the doctrinal/ethical disputes in 1 and 2 John and the organizational dispute in 3 John may be understood as two sides of the same coin. Though the emphases in each are different, they are both aspects of the same schism. As intriguing as this question is, however, restrictions of time and space do not allow me to give it treatment. It is my hope that this topic might be examined in a separate, future study. For the time being, it must be left to the side as I examine the question of 1 and 2 John.

---

48. Malherbe, "The Inhospitality of Diotrephes," 222–32.

IV

Applying the Model

Rhetorical Analysis

IF THE ANTHROPOLOGY OF religious schism is the exegetical vantage point from which I shall view the Johannine Epistles, then rhetorical analysis is the methodological approach by which I shall seek to bridge the gap between text and exegetical perspective. This choice is, in one sense, necessitated by the literary form of the text under consideration since the Epistles can be generally described as persuasive speech rather than, for example, narrative. While rhetorical criticism of the Johannine Epistles is in its nascent stages, some helpful research has been conducted by Duane F. Watson, and the methodological approach of Ben Witherington III's recent commentary on the Pastoral and Johannine Epistles is socio-rhetorical.

Both Watson and Witherington have classified 1 John as epideictic rhetoric, 2 John as deliberative, and 3 John as either deliberative or epideictic.[1] This classification serves as a helpful starting point for my

---

1. Watson, "Amplification Techniques in 1 John," 118; Watson, "A Rhetorical Analysis of 2 John," 109; Watson, "A Rhetorical Analysis of 3 John," 484–85; Witherington III, *Letters and Homilies*, 409–10. Stamps, "The Johannine Writings," 625, disputes Watson's identification of the Epistles' genres. Stamps argues that Watson's admission that 2 and 3 John are primarily epistles rather than pieces of rhetoric creates problems for proposing a rhetorical genre for these texts. "Rather, it is more likely that Watson has detected shared communication functions between letters and Graeco-Roman rhetorical convention. In this case, Watson's rhetorical analysis is insightful in highlighting the manner and style of argumentation but not in identifying the intended genre, structure and literary features of the Johannine epistles." Reed, "The Epistle," 176, however, argues that "it is reasonable to surmise that ancient letter writers could conceptualize an epistle in terms of 'accusation or defense,' 'expeciency or non-expediency,' and 'praise or blame' without necessarily being limited to the *genera* of the rhetorical handbooks . . . Epideictic was the most suitable of the three to the epistolary genre . . . A fundamental distinction between the epistolary and rhetorical *genera* is that the former were relegated to spatially-separated

interpretation. Three major categories for classifying rhetoric were first developed by Aristotle: deliberative, judicial, and epideictic. Each category has a specific setting envisioned: deliberative for use in political debate in a council or assembly, judicial before a judge or jury, and epideictic on occasions of public memorial.[2] Two subdivisions can then be formulated for each of the three major divisions: deliberative can be exhortation or dissuasion, judicial can be accusation or defense, and epideictic can be either praise or blame. Kennedy notes that Aristotle's tripartite division of rhetorical categories was not universally accepted, but it did have very wide acceptance and was certainly the dominant categorical breakdown.[3] Aristotle notes that there are some points of overlap in his categories when he observes that changing the form of expression can shift the category from deliberative to epideictic and vice versa.[4]

Watson's primary concern is not to argue for the classification of 1 John as epideictic rhetoric but to examine the role of amplification within 1 John. Nevertheless, since amplification is a characteristic of epideictic rhetoric, he briefly presents a defense of his classification.[5] Watson adopts Smalley's understanding of the purpose of 1 John: "The purpose of 1 John may therefore be summarized as *primarily* an appeal to the faithful: to strengthen the faith and resolve of true believers in the Johannine community by encouraging them to maintain the apostolic gospel."[6] This understanding Watson compares to Perelman, who says of epideictic rhetoric: "The purpose of an epidictic (*sic*) speech is to increase the intensity of adherence to values held in common by the audience and the speaker."[7] Besides an appeal to adherence to shared values, Watson also cites a present time referent, ascription

---

communication, limiting the extent to which they could parallel the typical oral, face-to-face context of judicial, deliberative, and epideictic speech. Some of the epistolary typologies at least functionally parallel the three rhetorical species, yet the epistolary theorists were not bound by a formal 'rhetorical' agenda for letter writing."

2. Mack, *Rhetoric and the New Testament* 34.

3. Kennedy, "The Genres of Rhetoric," 45. Kennedy cites Cicero, *De oratore* 1.16.35, 46-48; 2.39-43, in which Crassus takes the broadest view of rhetoric and questions "whether rhetoric is restricted to the law courts and assemblies." He also notes Quintilian, *Institutio Oratoria* 3.4, who notes that some authorities believe innumerable rhetorical categories to exist.

4. Cicero, *On Rhetoric* 1.9.36–37.

5. Watson, "Amplification Techniques," 118–19.

6. Smalley, *1, 2, 3 John*, xxviii; quoted by Watson, "Amplification Techniques," 119.

7. C. Perelman and L. Olbrechts-Tyteca, *The New Rhetoric*, 52; quoted by Watson, "Amplification Techniques," 119.

of praise or blame, and "stasis of quality" as further indications that 1 John is an example of epideictic rhetoric.[8] Witherington notes a common setting for epideictic rhetoric, and draws some conclusions from this for understanding the purpose of 1 John:

> Epideictic rhetoric is the rhetoric of, for example, funeral homilies, and in a sense our author is dealing with a post mortem situation. There has been a split in the Christian community, and some its (sic) members have been lost through their departure. Healing is needed, reassurance must be offered, and reasons to continue to embrace the fundamental values must be given because eternal life for the members of the community hangs in the balance.[9]

He then proceeds to refer to the opponents as "the departed" and argues that the homily is meant to help the community work through its grief and refocus its attention on their own "spiritual well-being and belief system." This may be pressing the funerary aspects of epideictic rhetoric too far. While the community has suffered the loss of some of its membership, this loss elicits not mourning on the part of the author but vitriolic attacks. The opponents are liars, murderers, and antichrists. The language seems closer to what one would find in a divorce court than a funeral parlor. Witherington is correct, however, in arguing that the overall function of the epideictic nature of the rhetoric is meant to shore up community identity and loyalty while also distancing the community from the beliefs and practices of the schismatic opponents.

While I agree with the categorizations offered by Watson and Witherington, I ought to note a caveat. Mack notes that a given speech might contain aspects of all six rhetorical subcategories,[10] that the very different social circumstances of early Christianity pose difficulties for the rhetorical categorization of early Christian writings,[11] and that full-blown epideictic rhetoric is not often to be found in the New Testament.[12] Indeed, aspects of both judicial and deliberative rhetoric can be detected in 1 John, and epideictic trends can be seen in 2 and 3 John. 1 John 2:12 is certainly meant to place blame upon the schismatics by associating them with Cain, but a forensic category is introduced by depicting them as murderers. The fine

---

8. Watson, "Amplification Techniques," 121–22.
9. Witherington III, *Letters and Homilies*, 431–32.
10. Mack, *What is Rhetorical Criticism*, 34.
11. Ibid., 35.
12. Ibid.

line between praise and counsel noted by Aristotle can also be detected, for one gains the distinct impression that 1 John is meant not only to solidify support that already exists, but also to persuade those who are wavering between the community and the schismatics that they should remain faithful to the tradition that they have received.[13] Similarly, one finds epideictic elements in 2 and 3 John. 2 John is addressed to ἐκλεκτῇ κυρίᾳ καὶ τοῖς τέκνοις αὐτῆς, and v. 3 is an example of both asyndeton and accumulation, both of which are amplification techniques used in epideictic rhetoric.[14] The point may be made best by examining 3 John. As noted above, Watson and Witherington are at odds concerning the rhetorical classification of 3 John, with Watson arguing that it is epideictic and Witherington arguing deliberative. A paradigm of the discussion can be found in 3 John 5-7, which is an excellent example of Aristotle's point that deliberative and epideictic rhetoric often differ only in their manner of expression. The Elder seems to write with the purpose of solidifying Gaius's support for the Johannine mission and persuading him to continue in his present course of action. This goal is achieved by praise for both Gaius and the Johannine missionaries; the missionaries are cast as honorable emissaries of Jesus Christ who have testified to Gaius's honor, and so Gaius should continue his honorable course of conduct and continue to support them. Diotrephes, on the other hand, has scorn heaped upon him for his dishonorable treatment of the missionaries. Surely Gaius would not want to align himself with such a reproachable figure. The vacillations between epideictic and deliberative rhetorical styles are evident: a decision has already been made, but tentatively. Therefore, Gaius must be persuaded to remain true to his decision. Rather than employ the proofs usually associated with deliberative rhetoric, the Elder appeals to ascriptions of praise and blame in order to persuade Gaius. The gist of these observations is that the categories offered by Watson and Witherington for understanding the Johannine Epistles should be used as heuristic tools rather than rigid definitions. Allowance must be made for the fact that elements of all three categories of rhetoric may be found in each Epistle.

A full examination of the specific rhetorical techniques employed in the Johannine epistles is beyond the scope of the present study,[15] but a

---

13. See, for example, 2:28.

14. Watson, "Amplification Techniques," 103, 114.

15. Such a study has already been conducted by Watson, "Amplification Techniques," and we will draw heavily upon his work as we examine 1 and 2 John.

few words moving forward should prove useful. It should first be noted that, much like rhetorical species, specific rhetorical techniques quite often overlap one another, and multiple rhetorical techniques may be detected together in the briefest of passages. Watson illustrates this point well in his examination of 1 John 2:12-14.[16] Both conduplicatio and expolitio are used in this single passage, Watson argues.[17] While I would not dispute Watson on this point, I would note for the sake of the present study that conduplicatio and expolitio are two very closely related rhetorical techniques. The former is "the repitition of one or more words for the purpose of Amplification or Appeal to Pity,"[18] while the latter is "dwelling on the same topic and yet seeming to say something ever new."[19] These two techniques then are not completely distinct from one another; their difference consists in the type of repetition that is occurring in each technique and the specific purpose intended. The significance of this for the present study is that multiple rhetorical techniques might be found being employed in the smallest of literary units, indeed, even the briefest of phrases. In addition, one's understanding of these literary techniques may be informed by one's understanding of the rhetorical category of the letter.

Finally, I might also make a general comment on some broader implications of rhetorical criticism for understanding the literary quality of the Epistles. The Johannine Epistles have occasionally been maligned as being of an inferior literary quality, especially when compared to the Gospel of John. Hengel has argued for such a position and uses it in part to reconstruct the circumstances surrounding the order and composition of the Epistles and Gospel. Houlden has been less restrained in maligning the Epistles, arguing that,

> No early Christian writing is so repetitious, so monotonous in its grammatical constructions, so narrow in vocabulary. The picture of the venerable elder, whom old age has endowed indeed with profundity of wisdom (Johannine fashion) but also with a natural incapacity to venture far in its formulation, is entirely understandable.[20]

---

16. Watson, "1 John 2.12–14 as *Distribution, Conduplication,* and *Expolitio,*" 97–110.
17. Ibid., 102–5.
18. Cicero, *Her.* 4.28.38.
19. Ibid., 4.42.54.
20. Houlden, *The Johannine Epistles,* 22.

However, the very monotony and repetition criticized by Houlden and Hengel are seen by rhetorical critics as hallmarks of good epideictic style. Indeed, Stamps, who is somewhat skeptical of Watson's detailed analyses of the Johannine Epistles, still notes that "the presence of such stylistic devices shows the linguistic artistry of the author . . . ."[21] It seems appropriate to note here before proceeding that rhetorical analysis of the Johannine Epistles serves to illuminate the skill and artistry of the author over against the assertions of incompetence served up by other interpreters.

The Use of the Gospel of John and Revelation

I have previously critiqued prior scholarship for its use of the Gospel of John in trying to reconstruct the beliefs of the opponents, yet I am about to incorporate not only the Gospel but also Revelation in my study of the schism in 1 and 2 John. Such a methodological move requires a word of explanation given my prior critique of it.

There is an important distinction that ought to be made between what I will do here with the Gospel and Revelation and what has previously been done with the Gospel. In prior research on the Johannine epistles, the Gospel tends to be used as a resource for reconstructing the beliefs of the opponents based upon what the epistolary author says about them. While such reconstructions may be helpful in a number of different ways, they are highly speculative when used for this particular purpose, for reasons noted above. My use of the Gospel and Revelation in applying my model to 1 and 2 John will differ significantly.

My approach in applying the model to 1 and 2 John is to move from the more general to the more specific. Thus, I will begin with some very general questions about the composition and ideological orientation of the Johannine community and move toward more particular questions regarding the process by which the schismatic dance is acted out by the epistolary author and the group that he represents. Ultimately, I will ask how the epistolary author goes about establishing the legitimacy of his position while undermining the legitimacy of the opponents and the rhetorical strategies employed to paint himself and his group as righteous and victimized by the unrighteous and deviant opponents. Before I do that, however, it will be helpful to reconstruct, as best I can, some more fundamental and general characteristics of the Johannine community for the

---

21. Stamps, "The Johannine Writings," 626.

purpose of reconstructing its general make-up, view of itself as a uniquely legitimate group, central theological identity marker(s), and past experience with schism.

To accomplish this task, it will be helpful to broaden my perspective as widely as I possibly can. For this reason, I will incorporate the Gospel of John and Revelation into my study. I will not, however, use these sources independently of one another. My hope is to compare the Gospel and Revelation with one another, and then to compare these results to the Epistles. In other words, far from using the Gospel and Revelation to construct speculative hypotheses, I am attempting to highlight patterns of thought common in all the texts of the Johannine corpus. As I move from the more general questions to the more specific, the Gospel and Revelation will fade increasingly into the background until they do not figure into the discussion at all.

The Johannine Community as Uniquely Legitimate

I have demonstrated in my model that a number of factors contribute toward the likelihood that a group will experience schism, and one of the most important of these factors is that the group understands itself as uniquely legitimate. However, I also noted that the contrast between uniquely and pluralistically legitimate groups is not an either/or dichotomy. Rather, they should be seen as extreme ends of a complex spectrum. I now turn to the Johannine community to ask where this group of early Christians fell on the legitimacy spectrum.

This question is complex and must take into account a variety of factors. A group may judge different ideological questions by different standards, thereby displaying traits of a uniquely legitimate group on some questions and more pluralistically legitimate on others. In the case of Temple Am Israel, Bayt Emmett's keeping of kosher was accepted by the rest of the Temple, but the *mechitza* was perceived as undermining the Temple's stance on gender equality, a belief seen as central to the Temple's identity by many of its members. Similarly, a group may respond in different ways to other groups, thus occupying different places on the spectrum depending on the outsider group in question. In the case of the Orthodox/Hicksite split within the Society of Friends, the Orthodox faction displayed a pluralistic orientation regarding mainline evangelical Protestantism and a more unique attitude toward the Hicksites. My investigation of the Johannine community in this regard will then require me to approach the question from a variety of angles if I am to attempt to judge the character of this group of congregations and assign them a general location on the unique/pluralistic spectrum.

It may be assumed *a priori* that the community was to some degree more uniquely legitimate since they are experiencing schism and uniquely legitimate groups are more likely to do so than pluralistic groups. However the community's central ideological beliefs must be identified, the claims around which this community's identity was formed. I will also need to gauge their reactions to a variety of other outsider groups. In order to give this aspect of my inquiry a maximum amount of breadth, I will include the Gospel of John as well as Revelation in my attempt to reconstruct the Johannine community's understanding of its legitimacy. In attempting to discern the central ideological identity marker for the community I will focus on its theology. Lastly, in reconstructing its views of outsider groups, I will examine Johannine responses to Greco-Roman religion,[22] Judaism, and non-Johannine Christians.

Jesus, in John 14:6, claims, "I am the way, and the truth, and the life. No one comes to the Father except through me." Appeal to this passage might be made at the very outset, with its seemingly highly exclusive soteriological claim, as evidence of both the Johannine community's sense of unique legitimacy and its central ideological belief. However, the meaning of this passage has been disputed in recent years. Our post-Holocaust theological context and increasingly pluralistic worldview have invited a re-examination of scholarship's understanding of John 14:6, and various proposals have been made that ultimately attempt to soften the seeming exclusivity of this passage.[23] From a methodological standpoint, the present

---

22. "Greco-Roman religion" will be used as a term inclusive of but not limited to the imperial cult, traditional public cults, and mystery cults. Aune, *Revelation* 2:765, notes: "Yet the primary issue reflected in the sources is not simply sacrificing to the emperor ... but sacrificing to the gods ..." This points to a certain degree of overlap between the various expressions of religious piety to be found in Greco-Roman culture. We find in the epistles of Revelation 2–3 an implicit critique of Greco-Roman religion as found in the trade guilds and explicit critique of the imperial cult (see below), but it is likely that the author of Revelation understands these as different expressions of a single reality.

23. This seems particularly true in studies where homiletical interests and the desire for interfaith dialogue are more prominent. O'Day, "John," 744–45, attempts to contextualize the passage within its first-century Johannine context, arguing that such a situation made it not simply understandable but permissible for John to make such a claim, but arguing that John's Logos Christology also allows for a more inclusive approach to theology.

study will be better served by a wider examination of the Johannine literature rather than depending upon a single contested passage of scripture from John's Gospel for reconstructing the Johannine attitude toward those outside the community.

As has already been noted above, and as has been discussed extensively in the secondary literature, the antagonists in the Gospel are "the Jews," and Gentiles (excluding the Samaritans of chapter 4)[24] get very limited mention. The most prominent mention of Gentiles in the Gospel occurs in 12:20–23, where Philip and Andrew bring to Jesus some Greeks (Ἕλληές) who had asked for an audience with Jesus. The passage is freighted with theological import as Jesus announces that this request signals the arrival of his hour. However, the Greeks themselves pass from the narrative without another mention, in a manner similar to that of Nicodemus in chapter 3. The incident does not give us the Gospel's assessment of Greco-Roman religion because these Greeks have come up to worship at Passover (so the partitive genitive ἐκ τῶν ἀναβαινόντων ἵνα προσκυνήσωσιν). This may indicate that these Greeks are either converts to Judaism[25] or "God-fearers."[26]

Sloyan, *John* 179–80, goes further than O'Day by arguing that this claim applies to Christians in a modern context, but only to Christians. It should encourage us to be missional in our faith, but it ultimately means that Jesus is the only way to God for Christians and not for peoples of other faiths. Culpepper, "The Gospel of John as a Document of Faith in a Pluralistic Culture," 107–27, reframes the question by arguing that contemporary discussion of John should focus on ethical rather than theological questions. See Barton, "Johannine Dualism and Contemporary Pluralism," 3–18, for a detailed critique of Culpepper's discussion. Charlesworth, "The Gospel of John," 259–75, argues that 14:6a may indeed be an historical Jesus tradition, but 14:6b appears to be redactional. Charlesworth implies that the redactional character of the most exclusive statement of 14:6 makes it less binding, if binding at all, upon Christians engaging in interfaith dialogue in a modern context. On the other hand, the majority of Johannine commentators would still seem to see this claim as a highly exclusive one. See Brown, *Gospel*, 2:630; Neyrey, *John*, 242; Smith, *John*, 268; and Witherington III, *John's Wisdom*, 249. The point of departure for the two sides regarding this passage seems to be that of the reader's ultimate goal. Those with hermeneutical concerns for the implications of this text for the relationship between Christians and non-Christians tend to downplay its exclusive characteristics while those with exegetical concerns seem to feel more comfortable with understanding the Johannine community as making a sweepingly exclusive statement.

24. The Samaritans, while we may classify them as Gentiles, cannot be said to be, on the whole, practitioners of Greco-Roman religion as we have so defined it. Unlike some other studies of the Johannine community (see Brown, *Community*, 35–40), the Samaritans will not play a significant role in this study.

25. So Brown, *Gospel*, 1:466.

26. So Moloney, *John*, 351; and Kossen, "Who Were the Greeks of John XII.20?," 97–110.

Either way, John presents them as somehow adhering to Judaism rather than Greco-Roman religion.

Of the Gospel, Epistles, and Revelation, Revelation displays the most obvious and negative evaluation of Greco-Roman religion, with Rev 13:14-15 giving us perhaps the most telling indications of this evaluation.[27] In these verses, a second beast causes the inhabitants of the world to construct an image of the first beast. The second beast then orders the people of the world to worship the image, and the image itself is animated by the second beast. It speaks and orders those who will not acquiesce to be killed. There is widespread agreement that these verses are inspired by and very likely directly reflect emperor worship in the late first century CE.[28] Price argues that the imagery of these verses is actually directly inspired by the erection of a colossal image of Domitian in Ephesus, and his proposal has met with approval.[29] If we have here a description of emperor worship in the Roman Empire, then surrounding remarks are telling for understanding Revelation's evaluation of this institution. Verse 7 depicts the beast as making war on the saints, while the previous verse has the beast blaspheming God. Most telling, perhaps, is v. 4, which reveals that the beast's power is conferred by the dragon, and the dragon is worshipped along with the beast. Revelation's evaluation of Greco-Roman religion depicts Greco-Roman religion, particularly the emperor cult, as antagonistic and hostile toward Christianity, blasphemous, and empowered by Satan.

Less prominently, but no less clear, is the presentation of idolatry in the letter to Thyatira, Rev. 2:18-29. In this letter, the Christians of Thyatira are rebuked for permitting Jezebel to teach φαγεῖν εἰδωλόθυτα. In addition, John associates this teaching with τὰ βαθέα τοῦ Σατανᾶ. The threatened punishment is that Jezebel will be thrown onto a bed of suffering and her "children" will be killed. A similar perspective is found in the letter to Pergamon, in which the church is condemned for holding to the teaching of Balaam, who encouraged Balak to entice the Israelites φαγεῖν εἰδωλόθυτα καὶ πορνεῦσαι.[30] Both depictions are associated with sexual immorality—a

---

27. Though, see also the letters in chaps. 2-3, and esp. 2:14, 20. That John argues against pagan religion generally and the Roman imperial cult specifically is widely accepted. See Hemer, *The Letters to the Seven Churches* 3-5, 7-8, 120-21.

28. Aune, *Revelation*, 2:761-65, Beale, *Revelation*, 710-15.

29. Price, *Rituals and Power*, 197-98. For agreement with this assessment see Beale, *Revelation*, 712.

30. For a full discussion of the issues involved with each letter, but particularly that of the Pergamenes, see Hemer, *The Letters to the Seven Churches* 87-94, 117-23. Hemer

common metaphor for idolatry—and both elicit God's divine judgment. The picture is of early Christian communities that have compromised themselves by eating food offered to idols, thereby provoking the anger of God and Christ.

The most apparent reference to Greco-Roman religion in the Epistles, 1 John 5:21, is a contested reference. Is the author actually referring to idols, physical depictions of pagan deities reverenced by the Gentile world, or have idols become a metaphor for the teachings of the secessionists?[31] Interpreting 5:21 as a reference to literal idols is a position once favored but has long since fallen by the wayside.[32] The majority of interpreters now favor some form of the metaphorical reading of "idols,"[33] and I agree with this conclusion. The primary argument against a literal reading of "idols" is the abruptness such a shift in topic would seem to represent. 1 John deals with matters of Christology and ethics, specifically the command to love one another, but nowhere prior to 5:21 does it address problems of the community's relationship to paganism. However, if "idols" are a metaphor for the things that separate humanity from God, in this case the teachings of the secessionists, then this closing line of the Epistle is actually quite a resounding rhetorical conclusion to the author's argument. It is in this very fact that the metaphorical use of "idols" becomes profitable to the

---

also sees a connection between the "teaching of Balaam" and the Nicolaitans, which may further add to the picture of the Johannine community as uniquely legitimate by incorporating material from the letter to Ephesus. However, I see no need to overcomplicate an already speculative use of Revelation in my reconstruction.

31. Brown, *Epistles*, 627–28, presents a far more complex range of options than the two we have presented here, and numbers ten possible interpretations of "idols." However, the majority of options presented by Brown can be understood as a sub-type of one of our options. In addition to our two options, a third possibility, represented by Brooke, *Epistles*, 154, is that "idols" would be inclusive of anything that takes the place of the worship of the true God. Thus, both physical depictions of pagan deities and the Gnosticizing teachings of the secessionists would fall under the category "idol."

32. Strecker, *Epistles*, 214, proves himself to be something of an exception here by associating "idols" with the sin unto death of 5:16–17. Strecker understands "idol" to be a way of referencing apostasy, particularly the apostasy of worshipping idols. In this way, Strecker has his cake and eats it, too: "idol" is a metaphorical means of referring to any sort of apostasy from the true faith, but the metaphor and its referent in this particular case are one and the same.

33. Brown, *Epistles*, 629; Bultmann, *Epistles*, 91; Smalley, *1, 2, 3 John*, 310; and Sugit, "I John 5:21," 386–90. A somewhat more nuanced reading is that "idol" has become a synonym for any kind of sin since Jewish thought so closely associated sin with the worship of idols. So Marshall, *Epistles*, 255–56; and Schnackenburg, *Epistles*, 263–64.

discussion of the Epistles' evaluation of Greco-Roman religion. The metaphorical understanding of "idols" might immediately seem to negate my use of this passage, but the fact that "idols" can be used by the author as a metaphor for the teachings of the secessionists actually demonstrates his low opinion of Greco-Roman religion. The epistolary author characterizes his opponents as liars, murderers, antichrists, and making God a liar. To equate such people and their teaching with Greco-Roman religion reflects the extremely negative evaluation of the latter held by the epistolary author.

The Johannine community, it would seem, does not allow for the legitimacy of Greco-Roman religion. While the Gospel of John does not directly address this issue, Revelation communicates a thorough-going rejection of Greco-Roman religion as illegitimate. Pagans are depicted as lethally hostile toward Christians and blasphemous toward God. The imperial cult is empowered by Satan, and the letters to Thyatira and Pergamon associate the eating of idol food with Balaam and Jezebel, two great villains of the Hebrew Bible. 1 John, while much more limited in its remarks, would seem to hold an equally negative evaluation of Greco-Roman religion in that it uses idolatry as a means of describing the despised opponents.

I now turn to what may be the most sensitive topic in all of New Testament studies: the Johannine evaluation of Jews and Judaism.[34] The discussion is wide ranging and covers the use of οἱ Ἰουδαῖοι, attitudes toward the mosaic law, and the use of Jewish scripture and symbolism. My goal here is not to exhaustively rehearse the options available on this particular topic, but to briefly examine the evidence and state my evaluation of the evidence as informed by those scholars who have devoted a great deal of time to engaging this issue. I will begin with Revelation and move to the Gospel. 1 and 2 John do not provide us with any concrete indication as to the epistolary author's evaluation of Judaism and so these two texts will not be addressed in this section.

Revelation displays a certain degree of ambivalence regarding Judaism. Perhaps the most striking indication of Revelation's evaluation of Judaism comes in the letters to Smyrna (Rev 2:9) and Philadelphia (Rev 3:9), where Jesus refers to the "synagogue of Satan" (συναγωγῆς τοῦ Σατανᾶ). The connection to Satan is strengthened by the fact that John refers to this group's

---

34. The attitude toward Jews and Judaism in Matthew's Gospel is also an area of sensitivity in our post-Holocaust context. The question of John's attitude toward Jews and Judaism has been the topic of a number of recent studies, including Bieringer et al., eds., *Anti-Judaism and the Fourth Gospel*; Hakola, *Identity Matters*; and Kierspel, *The Jews and the World in the Fourth Gospel*.

blasphemy, which is also characteristic of the satanically empowered beast from the sea in Rev 13:1, 5-6. The implication of such an identification is that John now understands Christians as the true Jews.[35] J. Lambrecht further argues that the connection between the Jews and Satan draws a parallel between Jews and Gentiles.[36]

Rev. 7:4-8 refers to the sealing of 144,000 drawn from a number of the tribes of Israel.[37] The unique nature of this list is well-discussed in the secondary literature and a full rehearsal is not necessary here other than to point out the complete absence of Dan and Ephraim, the presence of the tribe of Joseph alongside Manasseh, and the inclusion of Levi, which was usually excluded from catalogues of the twelve tribes in the Hebrew Bible. Of more pressing concern at the moment is the ethnic identity of the 144,000. Are they non-Christian Jews, Jewish Christians, Gentile Christians, or ethnically mixed Christians? Contemporary scholarship is rather united in its rejection of a literal interpretation of the 144,000 as non-Christian Jews.[38] However, there is some division over the question of a thoroughly Gentile group or a mixed group of Jewish and Gentile Christians. The notion of a mixed group is generally supported by arguing for a symbolic interpretation of the number 144,000: 144 is the square of twelve, which would represent the twelve tribes of Israel multiplied by the 12 apostles, and this is multiplied by 1,000, which was thought to be an immense number. This option may be exegetically tenuous, but the rejection of a literal interpretation of the 144,000 as non-Christian Jews is probably a rather safe conclusion. This would then constitute another example of Revelation's understanding of the church as the new Israel.

There is also in Revelation the use of cultic imagery to describe events in the heavenly throne room. While the vision of the New Jerusalem does away with the Temple (Rev 21:22), there is much imagery in Revelation to suggest that John has in mind a heavenly Temple or Tabernacle. 6:9 and 8:3ff both refer to an altar before the throne of God in heaven, and 8:3ff depicts an angel offering incense before God, the smoke of which is the prayers of the saints. 11:19, however, presents us with even more arresting

---

35. A commonly held interpretation of John's language here. See Beale, *Revelation*, 241; Lambrecht, "'Synagogues of Satan," 288-89.

36. Lambrecht, "Synagogues of Satan," 287.

37. On the nature of the partial list of tribes, see Smalley, *Revelation*, 184-86; and Beale, *Revelation*, 416-18.

38. See Beale, *Revelation*, 420-22; Harrington, *Revelation*, 98; and Smalley, *Revelation*, 184-88.

imagery. After a hymn of praise is offered to God by the twenty-four elders, the seer sees that, "God's temple (ὁ ναός) in heaven was opened, and the ark of his covenant was seen within his temple; and there were flashes of lightning, rumblings, peals of thunder, an earthquake, and heavy hail." Rev 15:5-16:1 gives an even more detailed description of the ὁ ναὸς τῆς σκηνῆς τοῦ μαρτυρίου ἐν τῷ οὐρανῷ, out of which come seven angels with seven plagues, and upon which descends the cloud of God's glory.

The picture that emerges is one of ambivalence. The Jews themselves fair rather badly under the withering criticism of the Revelator, but the institutions of second-temple Judaism seem to be viewed in a positive light, even if their validity is passing away in the light of the future establishment of God's eternal empire. This ambivalence is equally evident in the Gospel, though Christology plays a more prominent role in the discussion there.

A great deal of ink has been spilled over the issue of anti-Judaism in the Gospel of John, and my brief discussion here cannot hope to do it justice. Rather, I will attempt to sketch out some general observations by briefly focusing on three different aspects of the problem: (1) John's use of οἱ Ἰουδαῖοι, (2) John's use of polemical labels when referring to οἱ Ἰουδαῖοι, and (3) John's use of and attitude toward the Hebrew Bible and various symbols of Judaism.

The issue of οἱ Ἰουδαῖοι has received a great deal of attention, and a majority opinion seems to have formed in which this term is understood to refer to the religio-political hierarchy.[39] Charlesworth in particular presses this idea quite far, arguing that the term should be understood partitively: "*some* of the Judean leaders."[40] Charlesworth here demonstrates his incorporation of a second option. This option argues that the term should be translated as connoting geographical origins: the Judeans. However, this suggestion has not garnered as much support and has been criticized heavily by some quarters.[41] It should be noted that the "Judean" suggestion is complicated by the fact that the Samaritan woman at the well refers to Jesus as Ἰουδαῖος when he is said to hail from Nazareth in Galilee. This fact introduces us to a recurring characteristic of John's evaluation of Jews and Judaism: ambivalence. As Reinhartz noted above, there is no real consistency in the way that "Jews" are presented in John's Gospel. Jews are presented as

---

39. Brown, *An Introduction to the Gospel of John* 163–66; Charlesworth, "Exclusivism," 249–59.

40. Charlesworth, "Exclusivism," 257–58.

41. Aune, *Revelation*, 1:164, quoting H. Solin.

children of the Devil (John 8:44), seeking to kill Jesus, the source of salvation, comforters for Mary and Martha, believers in Jesus, and Jesus himself is called a Jew. Thus, there is evidence for a range of ways in which Jews are presented and a corresponding range of evaluations of Jews. They may be presented positively (salvation comes from them), neutrally (no negative or positive value seems to be attached to Jesus' identification as a Jew), or quite negatively (children of the Devil).

More disquieting than the label οἱ Ἰουδαῖοι is some of the vitriol hurled at the Jews by Jesus in their conflicts with one another. Particularly noteworthy is 8:44, where Jesus calls the Jews the children of the Devil, further characterizing the Devil as one who is a murderer, a liar, and does not have any truth residing in him. Characteristics of the father, in this case the Devil, are by extension attributed to the children, in this case the Jews (and Jews who have expressed belief in Jesus, no less!).[42]

John's evaluation and use of the Hebrew Bible and the symbols of Judaism is perhaps the most complex and extensively researched aspect of this problem and I cannot hope to fully reconstruct this wide-ranging topic in such a brief amount of space. However, I can lift up three specific instances of this phenomenon and thereby gain some insights useful for the present discussion.

John 1:17 reads: ὅτι ὁ νόμος διὰ Μωϋσέως ἐδόθη, ἡ χάρις καὶ ἡ ἀλήθεια διὰ Ἰησοῦ Χριστοῦ ἐγένετο. This relationship between the Mosaic Law and Jesus is one that plays into conflicts between Jesus and the Jews on several occasions in the Gospel. In John 5:1–18 and 9:1–41, Jesus' violation of the Sabbath by performing a miracle of healing becomes a point of dispute between Jesus and the Jews, with Jesus being called a sinner in 9:16, 24.[43] To violation of the Sabbath, S. Pancaro adds Jesus' identification of himself with God as a blasphemous violation of the Law,[44] as well as his false teaching that is opposed to the Law.[45] However, the Law is used by Jesus to defend his working on the Sabbath (John 7:21–24). Jesus also appeals to the Law's requirements concerning witnesses when defending his

---

42. Neyrey, *The Gospel of John*, 162.

43. Pancaro, *The Law in the Fourth Gospel*, 497–500, argues that John presents Jesus' entire relationship to the Mosaic Law through the lense of Sabbath observance. According to Pancaro's historical reconstruction, the Sabbath is not merely *a* precept of 2nd Temple Judaism, it is *the* precept and disregard for it is tantamount to disregard for the whole of the Law.

44. Ibid., 53–76. See John 5:17–18; 8:58; 10:24–38.

45. Ibid., *Law*, 77–125.

claims about himself (John 5:31-40). Following this defense from the Law, Jesus claims that Moses, through the Law, has condemned them (5:41-47). Thus, the Mosaic Law is presented in the same sort of ambivalent way in which "the Jews" is used as a label. It carries with it negative connotations in that it is used by Jesus' enemies as a means to accuse him (John 19:7), but Jesus uses it positively to defend his claims and actions.

In the Bread of Life Discourse in John 6, Jesus affirms the manna from heaven as a gift from God, but then proceeds to claim that he himself is the true fulfillment of this symbol of God's provision for God's people. The reference to manna would seem to be a multi-referential symbol that goes beyond simply recalling its appearance in Exodus 16.[46] In the literature of the early post-second Temple period, manna takes on eschatological and messianic significance. 2 Baruch 29:8 and Midrash Mekilta on Exo 16:25 envision the eschatological age as a time when manna will once again descend on God's people. Midrash Rabbah on Eccl 1:9 claims that the second redeemer will cause manna to fall just as the first redeemer did. While Brown expresses caution because of the later dating of these texts,[47] there are striking parallels between them and the way John seems to be presenting both the manna and Jesus in John 6. The eschatological expectation associated with manna fits well with the realized aspects of John's eschatology, and the messianic connotations obviously are good fits as well. However, the Johannine Jesus does not merely speak approvingly of these biblical and rabbinic themes in applying them to himself; rather, he exceeds them. They are a foreshadowing of Jesus himself. It is Jesus who is the true bread from heaven. The manna was eaten by the ancestors and they died in the wilderness, but the one who eats the flesh and drinks the blood of the Son of Man will never die.

A third and final example of John's use and presentation of the Law and the imagery of the Hebrew Bible can be found in his presentation of Jesus as the Passover lamb.[48] The theme is first introduced in 1:29, 36 and

---

46. See Brown, *Gospel*, 1:265–66, 272–74.

47. Ibid., 1:265–66.

48. The identification of Jesus as Passover lamb in John's Gospel is not without controversy. The primary points of dispute center around the interpretation of 1:29, 36; 18:28; 19:14, 29, and 36. Regarding 1:29, 36, Dodd, *The Interpretation of the Fourth Gospel*, 230–38, has argued rather strenuously that John the Baptist's identification of Jesus as the "lamb of God" is a reference to an apocalyptic lamb, but his argument fails to convince. A second possible interpretation of "lamb of God" is that it is representative of the suffering servant in Isa 53 (see Brown, *Gospel*, 1:60–61). Barrett, *Gospel*, 176, has

re-emerges in chapters 18 and 19. In contrast to the synoptic Gospels, John places the last supper and trial of Jesus on the day of preparation for the Passover (18:28; 19:14).[49] John then also conspicuously changes the timing of the trial of Jesus from one that occurs in the early morning (Mark 15:1 and Matt 27:1 place the trial before Pilate in the early morning; Luke 23:1 seems to move the time up a bit by placing the trial before the Sanhedrin in the early morning) to one that concludes at noon (19:14). While it is by no means certain, the timing of Jesus' condemnation would seem to correspond to the Mishnaic tradition regarding the timing of the paschal sacrifice when Passover falls on a Sabbath, as would be the case in John's chronology.[50] Adding to the overall picture of Jesus as Passover lamb is the use of hyssop to offer Jesus a drink (19:29)[51] and John's reference to Jesus' legs not being broken (19:36).

---

championed the paschal interpretation. Brown's attempt at synthesizing all three points of view by arguing that John the Baptist envisioned the apocalyptic lamb but John the evangelist intended the audience to understand a combination of both the servant of God and the paschal lamb is too nuanced. Against the paschal reading, some have argued that the Passover lamb does not remove sin, as John the Baptist's statements in 1:29 and 36 indicate. However, this assumes that the understanding of the paschal lamb articulated in the Mosaic Law was static and had not changed up to the time of the writing of John's Gospel. In fact, Ezekiel the Tragedian, *Exagoge* 185 and 190, refers to the Passover as a sacrifice that delivers the Hebrews from "these ills," and *Jubilees* 49:9, 15 speaks of the failure to observe Passover as leading to one being uprooted, while observance will prevent plagues coming to kill or smite those who observe the sacrifice. The point seems to be that sacrificing the Passover lamb was not merely a memorial of the passing-over of the death angel, but continued to serve in a very real way as a means of preventing evil befalling the one who sacrificed. We will accept here the paschal reading.

49. Köstenberger, *John*, 537–38, argues that John is actually referring to the day of the preparation in reference to the Sabbath, thus maintaining the Synoptic presentation of the Last Supper as paschal meal. However, John 18:28 rather strongly implies that the Passover had not yet been eaten, and 19:14 specifically refers to the day of preparation as being for Passover.

50. See Mishnah *Pesahim* 5:1: "The daily whole offering [of the afternoon] [generally] was slaughtered at half after the eighth hour [after dawn, about 2:30 P.M.] and offered up at half after the ninth hour [about 3:30 P.M.] . . . [If, however,] the eve of Passover coincided with the eve of the Sabbath [Friday], it was slaughtered at half after the sixth hour [12:30 P.M.] and offered up at half after the seventh hour."

51. See Brown, *Death of the Messiah*, 2:1076, for a discussion of hyssop. What is arresting about this particular image is the absurdity of someone using a flimsy hyssop plant to lift a heavy, wine-soaked sponge. Some have suggested that υσσοπος represents a corruption of υσσος, but Brown is correct when he notes that all other references to javelins in John are made with λογχη.

Applying the Model

The Gospel's presentation of the Law and various symbols of Judaism drawn from the Hebrew Bible is ambivalent, which is in keeping with other aspects of the Gospel's presentation of Judaism. The Law is never criticized outright. In fact, it testifies of Jesus. However, it is the Jews' Law, and not the Law of Jesus and his followers. The Sabbath is violated by Jesus, but he seems to do so in order to reveal his lordship over it. Manna and the Passover lamb are both used to reveal Jesus' character and mission, but the implication of the Gospel's use of term is that they are seen as having been fulfilled in Jesus. Jesus, not the manna, is the true bread from heaven. Jesus, not lambs, is the true Passover sacrifice. The Hebrew Bible points toward and prefigures Jesus, and his appearance has brought a better and more complete revelation of God to humanity. Thus, it would seem that John does not understand the Hebrew Bible, the Law, the manna, and Passover as bad or inferior, but, in a sense, passé. If Jesus has fulfilled that to which the forms and shadows pointed, then there is no more need to observe the forms and shadows.

Let us now return to John 14:6. Does this claim truly reflect an attitude of unique legitimacy over against first-century Judaism? The conclusion that I must draw from an examination of both Revelation and the Gospel of John is, "Yes." The Hebrew Bible and various symbols of Judaism are used by John, often in a very positive way. However, they are used to point to Jesus as their ultimate fulfillment. Revelation's depiction of a Temple-less New Jerusalem is perhaps the best depiction of this very fact. Revelation does not deny that the Temple was at some point in time valid. However, the climactic descent of the New Jerusalem to earth marks the passing of the need for such an institution. Similarly, the descent of the Son of Man to earth fulfills that to which the manna and the Sabbath and the Passover point, and so the need for these institutions has passed. Though modern readers might shy away from a supersecessionist theology, the Johannine community apparently did not.[52] When the Johannine Jesus declares that he is the way, the truth, and the life, and that no one comes to the Father except through him, he is making a claim that excludes both Greco-Roman

---

52. The implications of the Gospel's unique claims have been one of the more broadly and tendentiously discussed subjects of recent Johannine scholarship. For a variety of responses, see Culpepper, "The Gospel of John as a Document of Faith in a Pluralistic Culture," 107–27; a response by Barton, "Johannine Dualism and Contemporary Pluralism," 3–18; Koester, *The Word of Life*, 209–14; and Kysar, *John, the Maverick Gospel*, 159–63.

religion and Judaism as valid means of gaining access to God. But what of non-Johannine Christians?

Scholarship has held to a sectarian understanding of the Johannine community for some time now, though this position has come under increasing scrutiny in recent years.[53] I have noted above Hengel's understanding of the Johannine school as a distinct group within the Pauline churches of western Asia Minor. In this reconstruction, the Johannine school is understood to have been fully integrated into the mainstream of this region's Christianity, even if it would have been a distinctive and well-defined group-within-a-group. R. Bauckham has formulated an extensive argument against the position widely held in contemporary scholarship that the Gospels were written for particular communities and were not intended for wider circulation amongst other Christian communitities.[54] Given my argument for the existence of a distinctive Johannine community, it must be asked, in light of these criticisms, "What, if anything, can be discerned of the Johannine community's relationship with and attitude toward other early Christian communities?

The answer to this question will be tenuous at best for several reasons. The first such reason is that, unlike the question of the Johannine community's evaluation of Greco-Roman religion and Judaism, there are no apparent or direct references to non-Johannine Christians in any of the Johannine texts. Secondly, the indirect references that do exist are found in only one Johannine text, the Gospel of John (10:16 and 21:15-19), which places severe limitations on scholarship's ability to reconstruct the Johannine attitude toward other Christians from a plurality of Johannine texts. Finally, these indirect references in John's Gospel which might provide insight into the community's evaluation of non-Johannine Christianity are, at best, rather oblique and often dependent upon rather imaginative readings. *Despite* these cautions, I will proceed with an examination of these passages. *Because of* these cautions, my conclusions will be tentative and qualified in nature.

In John's Gospel, the first text that might draw attention is 10:16, where Jesus states: καὶ ἄλλα πρόβατα ἔχω ἃ οὐκ ἔστιν ἐκ τῆς αὐλῆς ταύτης· κἀκεῖνα δεῖ με ἀγαγεῖν, καὶ τῆς φωνῆς μου ἀκούσουσιν, καὶ γενήσονται

---

53. See Carter, *Empire* 8–10, for an overview and critique of the sectarian model. See also Barton, "Can We Identify the Gospel Audiences?," 189–93, who offers a strong critique of Meeks's seminal article "The Man From Heaven in Johannine Sectarianism."

54. Bauckham, "For Whom Were the Gospels Written?," 9–48; Bauckham, "The Audience of the Gospel of John," 113–23.

μία ποίμνη, εἷς ποιμήν. This enigmatic passage has received a level of interest disproportionate to its brevity, and three possible interpretations have emerged: (1) The "other sheep" are Gentiles, thus marking the expanding of an original Jewish-Christian community to include Gentile Christians;[55] (2) Jews in the Diaspora are in mind;[56] or (3) the "other sheep" are non-Johannine Christians.[57] The diversity of opinion by such able scholars ought to serve as a caution against too easily dismissing any of these arguments. However, one might argue that option (3) makes better sense within the overall narrative of John's Gospel and may work with John 21:15-19 to provide an indication of the Johannine community's relationship with other Christian groups.

Martyn manages to tie John 10:16 in with his two-level reading of John in such a way that this passage extends to other Christian communities the idea of the danger from the synagogue and Jewish authorities experienced by the Johannine community.[58] He argues that this passage is a brief allegory in which the other sheep represent non-Johannine Christians and the wolves represent the synagogue leaders who are seeking to expose Christians in as many synagogues as they possibly can. The hirelings who do not protect the sheep are the crypto-Christians who do not publicly profess their faith for fear of the synagogue leaders. John 10:12 indicates that the sheep have been scattered. The flock being addressed by Jesus in 10:16 is the Johannine community, so the other sheep must be other Christian communities who have been scattered because of the persecution by the synagogue leaders.

There are problems with Martyn's reconstruction, to be sure, such as his closely associating the scattering with John 11:52 when there is no scholarly

---

55. Bultmann, *The Gospel of John*, 383-84; Schnackenburg, *Gospel*, 2:299; Waetjen, *The Gospel of the Beloved Disciple*, 265; and Lindars, *Gospel*, 363. Fuglseth, *Johannine Sectarianism in Perspective*, 308, includes Barrett. However, Barrett's position ought to be qualified in relation to this particular understanding of the meaning of "other sheep." Barrett, *Gospel*, 376, explicitly identifies the "other sheep" as Gentiles, thus firmly situating the thought of the passage within the context of the Gentile mission. However, he closely associates the Gentile mission with a predestination theology that is closely associated with the Johannine conception of the incarnation. Theological considerations of this sort exclude *a priori* anything other than a missiological reading of the text.

56. Robinson, *Twelve New Testament Studies* 114-15; and Carson, *The Gospel according to John*, 390.

57. Martyn, *History and Theology*, 163-67; and Schoeps, *Jewish Christianity*, 131.

58. Ibid., 163-67. See also Martyn, "A Gentile Mission That Replaced an Earlier Jewish Mission?," 128-30.

consensus on the identity of τὰ τέκνα τοῦ θεοῦ τὰ διεσκορπισμένα in this passage. Further, Martyn again sees the scattering as effected through the use of the *Birkhat ha-Minim*, and I have already noted the problematic nature of this proposal.

Martyn's proposal tends toward the allegorical, and I would not follow him so closely as to see in this passage the sort of allegorical or encoded warning that he proposes. However, the general idea of the proposal is not without merit. I have argued above that there was indeed a rift between the Johannine community and its parent group, the synagogue. Given the caustic way in which Jesus describes the Jews in 8:44, the wolves of 10:12 may in fact be a reference to them. Again, given the sometimes caustic nature of John's evaluation of the Jews, it is difficult to imagine that τῆς αὐλῆς ταύτης is a reference to Jews or Jewish-Christians generally. The reference seems to work better as a describing a more limited group. But the other sheep are presented as already existing and on equal footing with "this flock." It would then seem possible, though by no means certain, that the "other sheep" are other Christian communities who are somehow separated from the Johannine community. What is notable for the present discussion is that John presents the flocks as in need of unification and does not seem to place any stipulations on this unification. If "this flock" is the Johannine community and the "other sheep" are non-Johannine Christians, John does not seem to view the non-Johannine Christians as in error or second-class in any way. In other words, John sees them as legitimate.

I now turn to the second of the two passages to be examined: John 21. The issues surrounding this chapter are manifold and complex. The overarching question that must first be addressed is the relationship of John 21 to the rest of the Gospel. It has become nearly universally held by modern scholarship that John 21 is a later addition to the Gospel,[59] and thus has become "the key and cornerstone for any redactional theory."[60] The arguments for John 21 being a subsequent addition to the Gospel are strong, and the real question seems to be not if John 21 was added later, but how much later was it added? A more pessimistic view is offered by Bultmann, who argues that John 21 is the later addition of the "ecclesiastical redactor,"

---

59. So Gaventa, "The Archive of Excess," 241. For brief discussions of the primary reasons for scholarship's rejection of John 21 as original to the Gospel, see Brown, *Gospel*, 2:1077–78; and Moloney, *John*, 545–46.

60. Smith, *The Composition and Order of the Fourth Gospel*, 234.

whose theology is markedly different from that of the evangelist's,[61] while a more optimistic assessment is that of Keener, who argues that John 21, while added later, was composed by whoever authored the rest of the Gospel.[62] The more specific question of common authorship of John 1-20 and 21 is not germane to the question at hand and is ultimately unanswerable. However, a more general question does bear directly on my present focus: Was this chapter penned by someone within the Johannine community? If the answer is "no," then John 21 is immediately irrelevant to the question of the Johannine community's attitude toward non-Johannine Christians. If the answer is "yes," then the present line of questioning may proceed.

The majority of narrative critical or literary studies of John 21 are not concerned with proving that John 1-20 and John 21 were both produced by a single author or community. Rather, John 1-21 are considered together in their canonical form, some sort of literary relationship being presupposed. The relationship between John 1-20 and 21 is then examined in light of this presupposition.[63] However, Culpepper argues that John 21 is "the necessary ending of the gospel," and "resolves some of the minor conflicts... and brings the development of John's symbols to a climactic finish."[64] Among the narrative elements that are tidied up in John 21 are the characterizations of Simon Peter and the Beloved Disciple, whose roles in the narrative future are filled in by alluding to the particular fate of each. No ascension is narrated as this event has been collapsed into Jesus' "lifting up." Instead, Jesus remains with the disciples in the end, seemingly a metaphor for the Paraclete's presence in the Johannine community.[65] Moloney argues that the presentation of Jesus in John 21 undermines the carefully constructed argument for the sacramental presence of Jesus despite his physical absence from the worshipping community.[66] Yet, Moloney is ultimately persuaded by the argument of Culpepper: "The one (or those) responsible for the epilogue of John 21 belonged to the same Christian community as the original

---

61. Bultmann, *Gospel*, 700–706.

62. Keener, *Gospel*, 2:1219–22.

63. John 21 has been researched quite broadly, with various aspects of its relationship to John 1–20 having been examined. For a substantial bibliography on the subject, see Moloney, *Glory Not Dishonor*, 184.

64. Culpepper, *Anatomy of the Fourth Gospel*, 96.

65. Ibid., 96.

66. Moloney, *Glory Not Dishonor*, 189–91.

author."⁶⁷ Indeed, while the evidence may not be strong enough to argue for common authorship, there do seem to be enough similarities in vocabulary and narrative tie-ins with John 1–20 to warrant the conclusion that John 21 is a product of the Johannine community and not an addition by a later redactor unaffiliated with the community's theology and heritage.⁶⁸

Having established the validity of the connection between John 1–20 and 21, I may now turn my attention to the treatment of Peter in this chapter, specifically, Jesus' words to him in vv. 15–17. In this passage, Jesus three times questions Peter's love for him, and responding to each of Peter's answers with an imperative: Βόσκε τὰ ἀρνία μου, Ποίμαινε τὰ πρόβατά μου, and Βόσκε τὰ πρόβατά μου. This passage is often associated by commentators with the Good Shepherd discourse in chapter 10.⁶⁹ It is not surprising, then, that this passage, like the Good Shepherd discourse, is seen by some as telling us something of the Johannine community's attitude toward non-Johannine Christians. Brown in particular argues that chapter 21 was written after the death of the Beloved Disciple and was intended to encourage Johannine Christians to reconcile with the Great Church, represented in this story by Peter. While Brown's reconstruction of the Johannine community can be and has been critiqued, there is a certain upside to his interpretation of this exchange. While the presentation of Simon Peter in John's Gospel is not negative, Peter is certainly placed in a role that is secondary to that of the Beloved Disciple.⁷⁰ In chapter 21, however, this presentation is altered. The Beloved Disciple retains his lofty position as witness and guarantor of the community's tradition (v. 24), but it is Peter who is charged with assuming the earthly role of Good Shepherd who, like Jesus himself, will lay down his life for the sheep. As noted above, the death of a movement's charismatic leader can and often does precipitate the dissolution of the movement. In the case of John 21, we may be seeing an attempt to preserve the community's integrity after the Beloved Disciples' death by urging the community to integrate itself into the Great Church. Like John 10, this implies some distance, whether geographical or ideological, between the

---

67. Ibid., 191. Moloney is more dependent upon Culpepper's argumentation in *John, the Son of Zebedee*, 297–325.

68. However, note Wahlde, *The Gospel and Letters of John*, 2:884–88, who sees the Gospel as having been composed in three stages, with chapter 21 possibly being an external written source adopted and adapted by the third "author" of the Gospel.

69. See, for example, Moloney, *John*, 555.

70. See Waetjen, *Gospel*, 15–25, for a comprehensive comparison of the characterizations of Simon Peter and the Beloved Disciple in John's Gospel.

Johannine community and non-Johannine Christianity. On the other hand, it demonstrates a willingness to accept non-Johannine Christians and to submit to non-Johannine ecclesiastical authority, even if the very fact that urging is necessary would indicate a certain degree of reluctance on the part of Johannine Christians to pursue such a course of action.

The evidence upon which such a reconstruction is based is, admittedly, slender, and one should not press these conclusions too far. However, if valid, they do offer a very fleeting glimpse of Johannine attitudes toward non-Johannine Christians. There seems to be some distance between Johannine and non-Johannine Christians discernible in these two passages. The exact nature of this distance is unspecified, and the two stories may even offer conflicting information. John 10 seems to imply a desire for unification with non-Johannine Christians while John 21 could be seen as reflecting more reluctance on the part of rank-and-file Johannine Christians for such a course of action. Such reluctance may mean that some, and perhaps most, in the Johannine community regarded non-Johannine Christianity as legitimate but inferior. Nevertheless, the fact that both passages indicate a desire on the part of the author(s) to unite with non-Johannine Christians would indicate that the community's attitudes toward Greco-Roman religion and Judaism did not extend to non-Johannine Christians, at least to the same degree.[71]

In summary, the legitimacy of Greco-Roman religion is completely denied by the Johannine community. Greco-Roman religion is in league with and empowered by the Devil and those who participate in it are in direct opposition to God. Judaism fares somewhat better in that its scriptures and symbols are understood as coming from God and pointing toward Jesus, but Jesus' coming to earth and being lifted up has fulfilled the types and shadows of the Hebrew Scriptures and its symbols. Therefore, it is not evil, but passé. On the other hand, Judaism post-Christ is sometimes depicted as being in league with the Devil, just as is Greco-Roman religion. These two institutions, Greco-Roman religion and Judaism, do not acknowledge Jesus as the only means of reaching the Father, and therefore they are illegitimate.

---

71. Of course, if some within the community really needed coaxing to join non-Johannine communities, then we have evidence of more complexity within Johannine Christianity with regards to its attitudes toward non-Johannine Christians. We would then have certain segments of the community holding to a less uniquely legitimate view that allowed for the legitimacy of Christians outside the community, while other segments would have held to a more uniquely legitimate view that was more reluctant to recognize the legitimacy of non-Johannine Christians. But again, this is highly speculative.

Non-Johannine Christianity, on the other hand, does acknowledge Jesus as such. Because of this, at least some in the Johannine community regarded non-Johannine Christianity as legitimate, even if some distance existed between Johannine and non-Johannine Christianity. Though the Johannine community cannot be classified as occupying the most extreme position on the scale of unique/pluralistic legitimacy, it would seem that the community was far closer to the unique end of the spectrum. Because of this, it would have had a low tolerance for certain ideological deviations within its ranks, thus making it more likely to schism.

I return now to John 14:6 and its highly exclusive claims. While modern attempts at softening the exclusivity of this claim may be commendable in their own way for our modern post-Holocaust context, it would seem that such an exclusive reading is consonant with the Johannine community's world view. Indeed, this passage does seem to reflect, generally, the Johannine community's evaluation of its own legitimacy and provides us with the community's central identity marker, and the standard by which it judges all outsider groups: its Christology. It is the community's aggressive Christological formulations that led to its separation from the synagogue, and the painful process by which it became separated from the synagogue firmly entrenched its Christology as the ideology by which everything is judged. Those groups (Greco-Roman religion, Judaism) who reject Jesus as Messiah are themselves rejected by the Johannine community. Other Christians who do not belong to the Johannine community are accepted, though there seem to be indications that some in the Johannine community viewed them as inferior. The schismatics have altered the community's traditional Christological confession and have apparently modified it to the point that the epistolary author cannot even regard them as being on the same level as non-Johannine Christians. Two further points need to be made in this regard: (1) The fact that a Christological controversy is contributing to the schism does not mean that such a controversy is the only source of conflict in the community. As I shall demonstrate below, a variety of other factors are feeding into the conflict reflected in 1 and 2 John. (2) The fact that Christological creativity on the part of the schismatics can be affirmed does not also mean that the precise nature of their Christology can be reconstructed, as I noted above. Scholarship must, in this case, content itself with a degree of uncertainty, acknowledging that Christology plays a central role in the schism while also acknowledging that the exact nature of the conflict is ultimately unrecoverable.

Applying the Model

A Heterogeneous Group?

Much like the question of the Johannine community's views regarding its own uniqueness, the question of the heterogeneity of the community must be answered by examining all of the Johannine literature. Specifically, I am inquiring into two aspects of the community: (1) the basic "ethnic" makeup of the community[72] and (2) if any socio-economic stratification is discernible in the community. In answering these questions I will assert that there is indeed evidence for ethnic diversity and socio-economic stratification in the Johannine community.

The question of the ethnic makeup of the Johannine community is not a new one. Indeed, Brown's complex reconstruction of the community's history incorporates two stages in which non-Jews become assimilated into the community.[73] However, let me begin basically by first establishing the Palestinian Jewish roots of the community and then moving to questions of the inclusion of Gentiles.

There is a strong majority consensus in contemporary Johannine scholarship that the Johannine community had its origins among the Jews of Palestine.[74] Martyn's entire thesis assumes that the origin of the community was in Judaism, and he further specifies that the Johannine community did not come "from the general world of Greco-Roman culture."[75] O. Cullmann's argument is much more specific and posits that the Johannine community first coalesced in Jerusalem and was composed of heterodox Jews such as the disciples of John the Baptist and the Hellenists of Acts 6–8. Brown disagrees with Cullmann, but is still able to affirm:

> J. L. Martyn detects in 1:35–51 that the Johannine community began among Jews who came to Jesus and with relatively little difficulty found him to be the Messiah they expected. I think he is perfectly right, and this challenges reconstructions of Johannine

---

72. I have in mind here two "ethnic" groups: Jew and Gentile. To be more specific with regard to the Gentiles, I have in mind primarily Gentiles who have come into the Johannine community from a background in paganism, though God-fearers and proselytes may have joined the community as well.

73. Brown, *Community*, 36–40, 55–58.

74. Langbrandtner, *Weltferner Gott oder Gott der Liebe: Die Ketzerstreit in der johanneischen Kirche,* is a recent departure from this position, arguing that the formation of the Johannine community post-dated the Jewish War.

75. Martyn, *History and Theology,* 149. Martyn does not rule out the possibility that John's Gospel was written in Alexandria (see 76n100).

history which would place the origins among heterodox Jews, among Gentiles, or among Gnostics.[76]

Waetjen argues for the composition of the Gospel in Alexandria, but also believes that the community that produced it was composed of former disciples of John the Baptist who had migrated there from Palestine.[77] These represent some very nuanced positions within the broader view that the Johannine community has its origins in Palestinian Judaism. Putting aside the more specific of these claims for a moment, let us consider the evidence for the basic assertion.

The literary evidence for a Jewish readership for the Gospel is so strong that Koester is able to say: "Jewish Christians were almost certainly at the center of the audience for which John's Gospel was written,"[78] and P. Borgen argues that it is "difficult to identify direct Hellenistic influence on John from outside of Judaism."[79] Indeed, there are very strong indications that the author and a good many members of his audience were Jewish. The author of John's Gospel seems to assume that the readers understand the various Jewish festivals such as Passover and Sukkoth, and, according to Koester, "can follow intricate debates based on the Scriptures and Jewish traditions."[80] The opening chapter of the Gospel also features a litany of Jewish themes that are not explained or contextualized for an uninformed readership. Jesus is presented as the Messiah who is foretold by scripture; the articular ὁ Χρίστος is consistently used, indicating that the author thinks of it as a "Jewish messianic expression" rather than as part of Jesus' name;[81] the titles "Son of God" and "King of Israel" applied to Jesus by Nathanael also recall Jewish tradition;[82] and Jesus is called "Rabbi" throughout the Gospel. These are all best explained by understanding the Johannine community as being predominately Jewish, but these ideas may be found just as easily in

---

76. Brown, *Community*, 27.

77. Waetjen, *Gospel*, 29. Waetjen also makes the imaginative but dubious argument that the Beloved Disciple was Lazarus (18–21). While I do not accept this argument, it does serve to illustrate that Waetjen identifies the Beloved Disciple as a Palestinian Jew.

78. Koester, *Symbolism in the Fourth Gospel*.

79. Borgen, "The Gospel of John and Hellenism," 116.

80. Ibid.

81. Ibid.

82. Ibid., 166.

Diaspora Judaism as in Palestinian Judaism.[83] What evidence might we find to indicate a Palestinian provenance?

Whereas Johannine place names were once thought to be symbolic,[84] contemporary scholarship, aided by archaeological discoveries, has come to realize that John's Gospel actually shows a familiarity with the geography of Palestine in general and with Jerusalem and its environs in particular. The pool of Bethesda is an excellent example of such an instance. John 5:1-3 describes the pool as adjacent to the sheep pool and having five porticoes. The late nineteenth century saw the discovery of this pool, a roughly rectangular structure enclosed by four porticoes and cut across by a fifth, confirming the Gospel's description of five porches.[85] Scobie, drawing on Kundsin, argues the Gospel's accurate knowledge of Palestinian geography would indicate that the Johannine community was:

> a community represented in Jerusalem though not part of the James-led church, a community which had engaged in a mission to Samaria and which included Samaritan converts, a community represented in certain locations in Galilee and Peraea but in rivalry with both other Christian groups and continuing followers of John the Baptist.[86]

While Scobie may take too great a risk in constructing a complex history of the Johannine community based upon geographical evidence, his basic point is well taken: the Gospel's familiarity with Palestinian geography would seem to indicate a Palestinian origin for the community. W. F. Albright also notes that John 3:23 is correct in both placing Aenon near Salim and noting the abundance of water in this location.[87] While avoiding the difficulties of accepting Albright's proposed Aramaic original of John's Gospel, Blomberg does concur with him in seeing the frequent use of Aramaic terms as an indication of a Palestinian origin for the community behind the Gospel.[88] There is no evidence that would dissuade me from concluding

---

83. By referring to "Diaspora Judaism" and "Palestinian Judaism" I do not mean to imply ideological differences. I merely mean to make a geographical distinction.

84. See Brown, *Gospel*, 44–45.

85. For a more detailed treatment, including further confirmation of the pool's identity from the Copper Scroll, see Blomberg, *The Historical Reliability of the Fourth Gospel*, 109.

86. Scobie, "Johannine Geography," 82.

87. Albright, "Discoveries in Palestine and the Gospel of St John," 159–60.

88. Blomberg, *Historical Reliability*, 27; Albright, "Discoveries," 157–58. Regarding

that the Johannine community had its origins in Palestine. Indeed, taken together, the Gospel of John's familiarity with Judaism and Palestinian geography serve as strong indicators that this is indeed the case.

However, the same kind of evidence marshaled in support of the community's Jewish character can also be used to argue for a Gentile component. The author's familiarity with Samaritan geography in John 4, noted above, coupled with Jesus' encounter with the Samaritan woman and the positive response to Jesus by the Samaritans is indication to some that there was a Samaritan component to the community.[89] Similarly, the Greeks' request for an audience with Jesus in John 12:20ff is seen as an indication that the Johannine community had broadened its horizons to include Gentiles.[90]

I have noted above my hesitation to place too much weight on such slim evidence. While I would not rule out the possibility of a Samaritan component in the Johannine community, I cannot fully endorse it in the absence of corroborating evidence. In the case of the Gentiles generally, however, there are other indications that the Johannine community had expanded to include them. The use of ῥαββί in John 1:38 is immediately followed by a Greek translation of the term, and "Messiah" is translated as "Christ" in 1:41. Certain Jewish practices require explanation, such as the use of stone water jars in 2:6. The addressing of the seven letters of Revelation to churches in western Asia Minor would seem to indicate a non-Palestinian locale for the Johannine community. In addition, the fact that emperor worship is an issue in these churches would seem to indicate a Gentile component since Jews were exempted from this practice. 3 John offers further possible evidence for a Gentile component in that all of the named individuals in this letter have Greek rather than Jewish names (Gaius, Demetrius, Diotrephes). Again, this is not conclusive evidence for a Gentile component. Indeed, some of this information could reflect a Diaspora Jewish component, and such a group surely must have existed within the Johannine community if it migrated out of Palestine, which seems quite likely. However, when taken as a whole, the picture is one of a community that had accepted Gentiles into its ranks. I may therefore say that the Johannine community was indeed an ethnically heterogeneous group, but

---

the Gospel's relationship to Aramaic, Davies, "The Jewish Background of the Gospel of John," is probably correct in noting that, while an Aramaic original to the Gospel is not likely, it is still "evident that John thought as a Jew. The Greek he wrote was influenced by a Hebraic-Aramaic idiom and connotation."

89. See Koester, *Symbolism*, 20–21; and Brown, *Community*, 36–40.

90. Ibid., 21–22.

what are the implications of such a conclusion for my understanding of the schism?

First and foremost, the heterogeneity of the Johannine community means that the epistolary author's declaration ἀλλ' οὐκ ἦσαν ἐξ ἡμῶν (1 John 2:19) must be taken seriously as an indication that those who eventually left the group had never managed to integrate into the group in a successful way.[91] Painter takes this statement as something of a rhetorical ploy meant "to lessen the impact of the schism on those who have been shaken by it."[92] By dismissing the schismatics as never really having been a part of the community, the epistolary author means to console and assure those who have remained. The majority of commentators, however, see in this statement a theological evaluation of the schismatics and their standing with both God and the community,[93] and Marshall and Bultmann even see an indication of the idea of the visible and invisible church.[94] This interpretation internalizes the significance and implication of this statement and the position is perhaps best articulated by Akin:

> The decision of the heretics to remove themselves from fellowship with the community gives evidence that they have never really believed the gospel and that their true inward devotion was to the world. John's reasoning in this verse is circular but flawless, given the presupposition that if they had been children of God they would have remained.[95]

The rhetorical and theological approaches to understanding this reference to the schismatics are neither improbable nor mutually exclusive. Painter's evaluation of the rhetorical function of this passage is consonant with the

---

91. Note that this is not a value judgment or an indication of some sort of failure on the part of the schismatics. Indeed, the structure and ethos of the Johannine community may very well have disadvantaged newcomers in their quest to integrate and become full participants in the life of the community.

92. Painter, *1, 2, and 3 John*, 204.

93. See Brown, *Epistles*, 339; Kruse, *Letters*, 102; Smalley, *1, 2, 3*, 102; and Strecker, *Letters*, 63–64.

94. Marshall, *Epistles*, 152: "Here is one of the clearest expressions in the New Testament of the way in which we must distinguish between the church visible, composed of those who outwardly belong to it, and the church invisible, composed of those whom the Lord knows to be his (2 Tim. 2:19)." Bultmann, *Epistles*, 37: "The statement permits recognition of the distinction between the empirical and the true congregation: false members are therefore to be found in the empirical congregation. The sentence is thus also an admonition to critical examination and certainly to self-examination as well."

95. Akin, *1, 2, and 3 John*, 116.

overall function of the letter, namely, to shore up group identity and prevent further defection, and this rhetorical purpose is achieved by means of the theological spin placed upon the situation (though the more specific view of Marshall and Bultmann smacks of an anachronistic projection of later Christian theological categories back onto this text and so should be rejected). However, while retaining both the rhetorical and theological explanations offered by contemporary scholarship, I would argue that allowance should be made for a reading that allows for some insights from the model of religious schism constructed above.

As I reconstruct the process of religious schism, a general and discernible pattern can be detected in which cliques form within a larger group, the cliques become disgruntled and become exit groups where members talk themselves out of the larger group, and finally the exit group becomes separated from the larger group either by expulsion or defection, thereby becoming a schismatic group. These cliques that eventually give birth to schismatic groups tend to form among group members who all share one or more common characteristics. If the Johannine community began as a Jewish group and then later accepted Gentiles into its membership, then two features are present that would have contributed to the formation of cliques within the community: (1) ethnic difference, and (2) newcomer status within the group.

If the Johannine community began in Palestine, then its composition would have been exclusively or nearly exclusively Jewish Christian. It would only have been later in its existence that it would have begun to bring Gentiles into its numbers. It is entirely possible and even quite likely that latecomer Gentiles were not able to assimilate fully into the mostly Jewish core of the community. This failure to assimilate would have manifested itself in an inability on the part of the newcomers to gain access to positions of leadership and power within the group because of their lack of knowledge of the community's tradition.[96] Further, their status as newcomers would have made them dependent upon the original members in a variety of ways. In order to acquire knowledge of the community's tradi-

---

96. It should be noted that 1 John 4:1–3 implies that the schismatics were involved in some sort of prophetic activity. However, this does not exclude the possibility that the schismatics did not have access to leadership positions, or at least the kind of leadership positions that they desired. It may very well be that their exclusion from leadership, to some degree, may have led to increased levels of prophetic activity in corporate worship as well as their "progressing" (ὁ προάγων) beyond the bounds of the community's theology (2 John 1:9).

tion, the newcomers would have had to place themselves in a position of dependence upon the original members. This may very well have fostered a sense among the newcomers that they were being treated as "second class citizens," giving rise to a sense of alienation. Secondly, the newcomers would have needed the original group members to extend hospitality and genuine acceptance to them if their integration was to be successful. The original members may have been, consciously or unconsciously, reluctant to provide such acceptance since doing so might mean the sharing of power and position within the community. In the absence of full assimilation into the community, a group or groups of Gentile Johannine Christians would have formed cliques. A continued and heightening sense of alienation from the larger group would have provided the impetus for the clique becoming a more closely knit group in which dissatisfaction with the larger group could be expressed, i.e., an exit group. Such expressions of dissatisfaction within a more insular setting may have led to reformulations of the community's Christological tradition, a central identity marker for the community. In a uniquely legitimate group such as the Johannine community, such reformulations would have served to speed up the process of separation already set in motion through the shift from marginalized clique to alienated exit group. Thus, when the epistolary author looks back upon the schismatics' time within the Johannine community, he is able to say, "They were never a part of us." Such a statement would surely have elicited agreement from many of the Epistles' hearers/readers as they recalled how the schismatics had never fully assimilated themselves into the group (even if the old guard had intentionally or unintentionally prevented full assimilation) and formed their own clique or cliques within the larger community.[97] Those who remained loyal to the epistolary author would have taken his

---

97. I am indebted to my colleague Wade Berry for pointing out a rhetorical critic might argue that such an obvious point would not merit mention in a rhetorical presentation such as 1 John. However, Berry counters that the average churchgoer can probably point to a number of times when he or she has heard a statement of the obvious that elicits the univocal approval of the addressees. One might argue that such a statement is itself a good rhetorical move designed to build group solidarity. An additional caveat is that the epistolary author my in fact be pointing out a fact that had not been previously noticed by the hearers/readers. The point of the rhetorical move is still the same, increasing group solidarity, but it is riskier in that the epistolary author believes that the hearers/readers will agree with him, but he is by no means assured that they will. He hopes that his statement will serve as an "aha moment" in which the hearers/readers suddenly realize the fact to which the author points. While either option (stating an already acknowledged fact or depending upon an "aha moment") is possible, it cannot be said with any certainty which the author intended.

statement as one of observable fact: the schismatics may have joined the community, but they never really became a part of it.

In addition to this ethnic heterogeneity, Klauck has argued that the Johannine community was economically heterogeneous. Klauck understands 1 John 4:5 as indicating that the opponents had done a better job of coming to terms with the non-Johannine "world" than had the rest of the community.[98] This in part involved the opponents' acquisition of material goods, which the epistolary author criticizes in 1 John 2:16 and 3:17.[99] The opponents, as Klauck reconstructs them, counted more of the well-off members of the community among their numbers. The withdrawal of the opponents then meant the withdrawal of the financial support they lent the community in the form of meeting places, meals, and the extension of hospitality to itinerant preachers.[100]

Such a reconstruction is based upon mirror-reading the text and caution should be exercised in accepting it. However, it is commendable in more than one way. As noted above, 1 John demonstrates a strong concern for love of the community members. This lack of love is given concrete expression in 3:17. The question here is not one of love for an outsider, but of love for fellow community members, brothers and sisters.[101] In the author's scenario, one who has the world's goods (τὸν βίον τοῦ κόσμου) sees a brother or sister in need and withholds material provision from him or her. The love of God, so the author says, does not abide in such a person. This assertion is part of a larger rhetorical unit of vv. 11-19, which reminds

---

98. Klauck, "Internal Opponents," 56. What is significant here is that those who are of the world seem to be identified here with those who have a spirit that does not confess that Jesus Christ came in the flesh. This would then suggest that Klauck is correct in understanding that those who are of the world should be identified with the opponents.

99. Ibid., 56.

100. Ibid., 57. Brown, *Epistles*, 475, seems to agree with Klauck's basic proposal regarding economic disparity when he notes that the author's insistence upon this communal care "makes sense if the secession has created a problem of need so urgent that the author may well think it reflects the last hour. The passage raises the *possibility* that the members of the Johannine community with 'enough of this world's livelihood' (3:17a) had joined the secession, leaving the author's adherents in dire need." Smalley, *1, 2, 3 John*, 196, argues that the phrase τὸν βίον τοῦ κόσμου does not necessarily refer to an abundance of wealth, but merely what someone would ordinarily be expected to possess. Still, he connects 3:17 with 1 John 2:16 and allows that this conjunction "may suggest that the idea of luxury is not entirely excluded from the term as it occurs in the present v, even if its meaning is by no means exhausted as a result."

101. *Pace* Smalley, *1, 2, 3 John*, 196-97, who argues that this is a general admonition that need not be restricted only to members of the Johannine community.

Applying the Model

the community of the commandment that the community has had from the beginning: community members should love one another. This rhetorical unit does not follow the general pattern of rhetorical argumentation.[102] It begins with a statement of the case: the community should observe the commandment that it has had from the beginning that the community members should love one another. However, the second rhetorical move that one should expect, the immediate defense of the position by means of a syllogism, is absent. Instead, the reader is immediately presented with an example of antithesis[103]: Cain is presented as a contrast to the type of behavior urged by the epistolary author. v. 13 then draws parallels between the world and Cain on the one hand, and the community and Abel on the other. The implication of this parallel is that the world is unrighteous and the community is righteous. But one might take the parallel even further and ask if the author intends his hearers/readers to understand some relationship between themselves and world that might parallel that of Cain and Abel. The author may very well be telegraphing to his audience that he will be indicting the schismatics. They were once brothers and sisters, but have, in essence, butchered (ἔσφαξεν) the community members in the act of separation just as did Cain against Abel. V. 14 sees a brief departure from the theme of murder (though the themes of life and death remain quite prominent) with the chiastic assertion that the community knows it lives because it loves, while those who do not love do not live. V. 15, taken with 14b, is an example of *expolitio*, which Cicero defines as "dwelling on the same topic and yet seeming to say something ever new."[104] The basic idea of 14b is emphasized in stronger terms in v. 15: no longer is the subject described as the one who does not love, but the one who hates and so is a murderer (like Cain). No longer does such a one remain in death; rather, eternal life does not dwell in such a person. In contrast to this is the historical example of Jesus, who laid down his life for the community. Rather than following the example of Cain, Jesus is urged as the example to follow. It is Jesus who demonstrates love through his own death, rather than hatred by inflicting death on others. The concept of laying down one's life is then extended to sacrificing one's material possessions for the benefit of another

---

102. See Mack, *Rhetoric*, 40, for this three-part pattern in classical rhetorical argumentation.

103. On antithesis, see Watson, "Amplification Techniques," 115.

104. *Her.* 4.42.54. Watson, "Amplification Techniques," 103–4, understands *expolitio* as being formed by "repeating the same idea in different form or by altering it."

in v. 17. This verse by itself, while accusatory, does not seem to be a terribly aggressive rhetorical move. It merely asserts that one's inner disposition is revealed through outward behavior: those who have God's love abiding in them will demonstrate this by sharing their worldly possessions with other members of the community. Those who do not have God's love abiding in them will not share their material goods with other members of the community. However, the rhetorical context adds more gravity to this charge. In a typically Johannine fashion, two opposing attitudes have been draw up: love or hate. The one who does not share his or her possessions with needy members of the community must hate the needy members of the community. Those who hate (1) do not have eternal life, (2) remain in death, and (3) are murderers. The example of murder given at the very beginning of this passage is Cain, who committed not simply murder, but fratricide. The rhetorical unit then closes with an exhortation to love in deed and in truth (ἔργῳ καὶ ἀληθείᾳ).

The epistolary author has structured the unit so that the exhortation to share one's possessions with other members of the community is set in sharply dualistic tones. Sharing indicates that one either loves or hates, abides in life or death, follows the example of Jesus or of Cain. The last point reinforces the idea that a setting within the Johannine community is envisioned. The generic ἀλλήλους of v. 11 very quickly gives way to repeated emphasis on the love of the brothers and sisters (ἀδελφοί) in vv. 14, 15, 16, and 17. One cannot help but notice that the author twice emphasizes that Cain slew his ἀδελφός.

One is left with the impression that Klauck has made a valid point when he argues that there are economic disparities in the Johannine community and that they are playing into the schism. However, let me make a few observations. Brown's caution that this scenario is a *possibility* is a good one. Again, the reader is being given only the author's point of view. To extrapolate from this that the schismatics were extremely wealthy and had previously engaged in providing benefits to the community but had ceased to do so is stretching the evidence farther than it can go. What can be said is that the epistolary author appears to see the schismatics as having material goods that are unavailable to the rest of the community. If such a disparity did indeed exist, it need not follow that the schismatics had ceased to provide material support to the community. Indeed, the author's complaint may very well have been a long-standing one. With such uncertainties regarding the historical situation, what can be said about the implications for these perceived economic disparities' impact on the schism?

If economic disparities did exist in the community, and the wealthy tended to side with the schismatics, then I can affirm that economic heterogeneity contributed to the disintegration of the community. If the schismatics were wealthy Gentiles who had only recently come into the community, then their sense of alienation from the Jewish core group may very well have been greater than what they would have experienced had they been economically disadvantaged. Poorer newcomers most likely would not have expected to take on high-status positions within the group, but wealthier newcomers may very well have expected to receive the same sort of treatment afforded them by "the world" based on their economic status. Their expectations would have set them up for alienation, almost dooming the Johannine community to a schismatic fate when it allowed these wealthy Gentiles into the community. In this case, they may have either offered their material wealth to the community as a means of trying to achieve a higher status within the group, or they may have withheld such support as a means of gaining leverage on the community's leadership. In the former case, their support would have been withdrawn when they exited the community, thus eliciting the harsh reaction from the epistolary author. This scenario would imply that the economic heterogeneity of the group contributed to the schism by heightening the schismatics' sense of alienation from the group, thus hastening their departure. Economic heterogeneity would not have impacted the epistolary author as a factor in the schism until after separation occurred and material support for the community was withdrawn. In the latter case, the presence of wealthy members who would not contribute to the material well-being of the group may have resulted in pressure being applied to the wealthy by the epistolary author and the Jewish core group. The author and his followers may have become more of a closed group in reaction to the resistance of the Gentiles, thus further denying Gentiles the status within the group that they so desired. In this case, the community's economic heterogeneity was a factor in both sides' drive toward separation and the epistolary author's mention of it in 1 John is nothing new.

But what if the schismatics were not wealthier than the Jewish core group, or at least were not as wealthy as the epistolary author seems to believe? In other words, what are the implications of the epistolary author's *mistaken perception* of economic heterogeneity? The way the course of events plays out in this scenario is not radically different from what I noted above. The epistolary author and his followers would have expected material provision from these newcomers that they simply were not able to provide. For this reason, the author and his followers close ranks and refuse to allow the newcomers to fully assimilate into the group, thus compounding the problems presented by the ethnic heterogeneity of the group. In this case, the tensions originate on the side of the epistolary author and his followers.

I would argue that economic heterogeneity played a role in the schism in that, at the very least, the epistolary author believed such heterogeneity to be real. Even the perception of economic disparity would be enough to cause tensions in the community. However, it might also be asked how this perception arose if there were no reality behind it? The schismatics may indeed have been materially better off than the author and his followers, though they may not have been so much better off that they felt able to provide for the needs of others within the community.

Arguing for Legitimacy

I have argued thus far that the Johannine community was a uniquely legitimate group that denied the legitimacy of Greco-Roman religions as well as Judaism, and seems to have had an ambivalent attitude toward non-Johannine Christianity. There was some distance (geographical? theological?) between the Johannine community and non-Johannine Christianity, though John 10 and 21 seem to indicate that some in the community were attempting to overcome this distance and to seek closer communion with non-Johannine Christianity. The community had previously experienced a schism with the synagogue, the primary impetus for this separation being the Johannine community's increasingly high Christology. As a result of this hard-fought period in the community's history, its Christology had become its central identity marker and its uniquely legitimate views of itself were inextricably bound to its view of Jesus Christ. To deviate from the community's tradition in this regard was to invite a harsh reaction.

The community was heterogeneous in several ways. It began as a Palestinian Jewish group that at some point migrated out of Palestine, probably into western Asia Minor. It began to accept Gentiles into its ranks—likely after settling in Asia Minor—and this began a process of stratification within the community along lines of ethnicity and length of membership. These newcomer Gentiles found it difficult to assimilate into the old Jewish core group and so experienced a sense of alienation. This sense of alienation was heightened by some economic disparity (or perception thereof) between the Jewish core group and the Gentile newcomers. This sense of alienation allowed for the formation of a clique or cliques on the part of the Gentile members, who began to revise the community's Christological tradition in some way. This revision, not unexpectedly, led to a harsh reaction from the epistolary author and his followers and separation ensued. It is probably at this point that 1 and 2 John are composed. The separation has, at the very least, begun, for the epistolary author is able to speak of the separation as a past event (1 John 2:19 and 2 John 7). In writing 1 and 2 John, the epistolary author is attempting, at least in part, to re-establish the legitimacy of himself and his followers and their interpretation of the community's tradition. The question which must now be addressed is how did the epistolary author go about doing this? The primary answer to this question is that the epistolary author attempts to establish his legitimacy over against the illegitimacy of the opponents. The epistolary author's attempt to establish his own legitimacy is best seen, I believe, in 1 John 1:1–3, and the epistolary author's appeal to the Spirit in 1 John 4:1–6.

In 1 John 1:1–3, fellowship with God and God's son is predicated upon the addressees' fellowship with a nebulous "we", and this assertion is based upon the fact that "we" have heard, seen with their eyes, and handled with their hands the very message that they are proclaiming to the addressees. The issues surrounding this particular pericope are complex and often stray outside the bounds of the interests of the present study. Two issues ought to be addressed before moving forward, however: (1) the issue of the identity of the epistolary author, and (2) the question of the referent of the oft-repeated ὅ. Regarding the latter, I think it best to agree with Witherington that Jesus, "God's wisdom come in the flesh,"[105] is the referent. Such an identification sets the stage for the rest of the epistle. The author immediately begins by stating his relationship to Jesus Christ. Regarding the former, a specific answer to this question, i.e., an attempt to identify the epistolary author with a known figure in early Christianity, is less pressing. The question of a specific author is immaterial to the questions of the present study. However, this question does provide a segue into one that is more pressing.

---

105. Witherington III, *Letters and Homilies*, 440.

The language of vv. 1-4 is that of sensory perception. The author employs a series of relative clauses in the perfect and aorist tenses to describe Ὅ ἦν ἀπ' ἀρχῆς:_ ἀκηκόαμεν, ἑωράκαμεν, ἐθεασάμεθα, and ἐψηλάφησαν. Moreover, these sensory perceptions are connected with the bodily means by which such perception is achieved: τοῖς ὀφθαλμοῖς and αἱ χεῖρες. This would seem to be a straightforward claim to an eyewitness encounter with the historical Jesus. However, such a claim has been disputed by many contemporary scholars. A number of scholars who tend to be of a more conservative persuasion have no difficulty with accepting this as a claim to eyewitness testimony, though they do not all necessarily understand the author to be the Beloved Disciple, whatever his historical identity may be.[106] On the other hand, others deny that this is the language of eyewitness testimony.[107] Such a position is generally taken because a prior determination has been reached regarding authorship in which an eyewitness to Jesus' ministry has been excluded from the discussion, usually on the basis that the Epistles are to be dated so late in the first century that an eye-witness surviving so long is deemed improbable. This passage is then seen as posing something of an obstacle that must be navigated, and the solutions to the problem tend toward the creative, with none of the proposals having garnered widespread acceptance.

---

106. Kruse, *Letters*, 52; Smalley, *1, 2, and 3 John*, xxii, 8; does not directly address the question but leaves open the possibility that John the Apostle is the author of the Epistles, thereby allowing for the language of eyewitness in 1:1-4; Smith, *First, Second, and Third John*, 18, sees 1:1-4 as speaking of a "firsthand relationship with Jesus"; Thompson, *1–3 John*, 35–36, allows that the author speaks as an eyewitness; Stott, *Letters*, 64–66; Robert W. Yarbrough, *1–3 John*, 5–15, 35–38.

107. Brown, *Epistles*, 158-63 (though see the rebuttal of Kruse, *Letters*, 53–56, and Schnackenburg, *Epistles*, 54–55. Kruse at times overstates his case, but he does effectively demonstrate that Brown does so as well); Bultmann, *Epistles*, 7–12; Houlden, *Epistles*, 48; Johnson, *1, 2, and 3 John*, 26; Marshall, *Epistles*, 101–3, does not explicitly disallow eyewitness testimony but focuses so intently on providing a theological rationale for the language that he does so implicitly; Painter, *1, 2, and 3 John*, 130; Rensberger, *1 John, 2 John, 3 John*, 46–47; Schnackenburg, *Epistles*, 52, 56, argues that the language of sensory perception cannot be taken literally because such an historical concern is at odds with the author's concern for "the divine veiled in earthly vesture." Rather, he sees sees 1:1-4 as a theological argument meant to contradict the Docetism of the opponents, with the sensory language employed to emphasize the reality of the incarnation. Strecker, *Letters*, 13–14. Black, "The First, Second, and Third Letters of John," 365–66, and 382, avoids the subject altogether by arguing that the identity of the epistolary author is a mystery to us and by simply stating that 1 John 1:1 is a theologically motivated emphasis on Jesus' humanity.

Applying the Model

Bultmann explains the sensory language of v. 1 by arguing that the author is speaking of both an historical and an eschatological reality. It is the eschatological reality to which he primarily refers and does so with the language of sense perception in order to contradict the opponents and their docetically inclined theology.[108] Strecker argues that the language of sensory perception is a case of an "indirectly expressed" pseudepigraphy[109] that is meant to create the impression that the author is an eye-witness to the incarnation, again, in order to refute the Docetic Christology of the opponents. Schnackenburg proposes that the author is making a theological argument. The author is concerned with refuting the opponents by asserting the reality of the incarnation and so employs the language of sensory perception in order to reinforce the reality of an historical incarnation. Brown argues that the use of eye-witness language when the author was indeed not an eye-witness is not uncommon in contemporary literature, and its use in 1 John 1:1 "goes beyond a covenant identification with the first generation. It helps to authenticate the interpretation of the Johannine tradition that will be presented in I John."[110] Painter argues that the language is that of firsthand testimony, but only as it is accessed by those who have received the tradition from these witnesses. In other words, the appeal is to actual eye-witness testimony, but it is not the eye-witness testimony of the author.[111]

There is a good deal of disagreement, then, on how one should understand 1 John 1:1. On the one hand, some scholars see it as the author's appeal to his own testimony as an eye-witness. On the other hand there are those scholars who deny that the author is an eye-witness, but cannot agree on an alternative understanding of the language. What insight can be gained by reading this verse in light of my model of religious schism? An initial analysis based on rhetorical criticism will set the stage for understanding this passage as an attempt to establish a form of legitimacy which the schismatics cannot access. In other words, the epistolary author[112] is

---

108. Bultmann, *The Johannine Epistles*, 10–11.
109. *Letters*, 14.
110. Brown, *Epistles*, 161.
111. *1, 2, and 3 John*, 135.

112. I will treat here an issue that arises in the literature on 1:1–5: The use of the first-person plural. 1 John seems to use the first-person plural in a variety of ways. It is used here to set the "we" of the sender or senders over against the "you" of the recipients. This usage seems to be without parallel in the rest of the epistle. This contrasts with 1 John 4:14, where the author seems to use the first-person plural to include the recipients,

attempting to cast his position as uniquely legitimate and that of his opponents as illegitimate.

The rhetorical handbooks offer a very clear picture of the accepted function of the opening of a rhetorical piece.[113] This prologue, *exordium*, is intended "to establish the desired relationship with one's audience; this is generally held to entail rendering them attentive, receptive and well-disposed."[114] These goals are attained by establishing the *ethos*, or character, of the rhetor.[115] Cicero's discussion of the *exordium* is particularly helpful in that he discusses it according to various types of cases to which the rhetor must speak.[116] Among these are the honorable, difficult, mean, ambiguous, and obscure. Of the five options, 1 John seems to fall best into the category of the ambiguous case, which Cicero defines as, "one in which the point for decision is doubtful, or the case is partly honourable and partly discreditable

---

and such a usage is recurrent throughout the epistle. On the other hand, 1:6 is generally seen as using "we" to denote a slogan used by the schismatics. This usage parallels such passages as 2:4 and 6, with their use of ὁ λέγων ὅτι and 2:23 with its use of πᾶς ὁ ἀρνούμενος. As I shall note below, some scholars take the usage in 1:1-5 quite literally, understanding the author as writing on behalf of a circle of leaders or teachers within the community who can join with the epistolary author in claiming the same experience. In the case of those scholars skeptical of eye-witness claims in 1 John 1:1-4, the "we" then refers to second- or third-generation Christians who appeal to their community's tradition, which may have some basis in the testimony of one or more eye-witnesses. For those more optimistic about eye-witness testimony, the "we" is often equated with a reference to the Apostles (see Yarbrough, *1-3 John*, 33-34). However, such a reading is complicated by the fact that the epistolary author then shifts to the first-person singular (1 John 2:1, 12-14, for example), which he uses with a good deal of consistency throughout the rest of the epistle. I will take the position here that the "we" of 1:1-4 is something more of a regal plural or plural of modesty. Such a phenomenon is not unknown in classical literature generally or in the New Testament specifically. Melherbe, *The Letters to the Thessalonians*, 86-89, takes the position that the first-person plurals of 1 Thessalonians are an example of such a literary convention, which was also evidenced in Seneca, and that this position is supported by patristic interpretations of 1 Thessalonians. The fluid use of the plural, the apparent lack of its use to create distance outside of 1:1-5, and the use of the singular when the author addresses the recipients would indicate to me that the plural in 1:1-5 ought to be viewed as a literary device rather than an actual reflection of a plurality of senders who stand with the epistolary author as witnesses.

113. Witherington III, *Letters and Homilies*, 437-46, is the only commentator that I have found who fully appreciates the rhetorical nature of 1 John 1:1-4. Following his lead, I understand this passage to be a rhetorical prologue, or *exordium* or *proemium*.

114. Malcolm Heath, "Invention," 103.

115. Mack, *Rhetoric*, 36.

116. *Inv.* 1.20.

so that it engenders both good-will and ill-will."[117] He goes on to describe the approach that one should take when constructing the *exordium* for an ambiguous case: "If an ambiguous case has a doubtful point for the judge's decision, the exordium must begin with a discussion of this very point. But if the case is partly honourable and partly discreditable, it will be proper to try to win good-will so that the case may seem to be transferred to the honourable class."[118] Of the two options proposed, the former seems to best fit the situation in 1 John and the point at which the epistolary author is driving. The crux of the matter, which may be lost in the Christological and ethical debate as it unfolds in 1 John, is the hearer's standing with God. Should the hearer take the erroneous side of the schismatics, his or her right standing before God is lost. On the other hand, should the correct tradition represented by the epistolary author be chosen, then one's standing before God is preserved.[119] Stating the question in such a way also serves the purpose of piquing the interest of the hearer.[120] According to Quintillian's views on the purpose of the prologue, a third function is served: preparing the audience to receive instruction.[121] By constructing the *exordium* in such a way that the stakes are raised so highly, the epistolary author hopes not only to gain the attention of the hearers, but to cause them to be receptive to his argument. But, having made so much contingent upon the hearer's association with himself, how does the epistolary author justify the extravagant claims that he has made?

    It is at this point that I turn from classical rhetoric and toward religious schism as a means of understanding what the epistolary author is doing in 1 John 1:1-4. The author has implicitly drawn a very stark contrast. He has plainly stated that association with himself is the only means for the hearer to be associated with God (thus reflecting his uniquely legitimate mindset).

---

    117. Ibid. Contrast this with categorizations of *Rhetorica ad Herennium* 1.5, which breaks the various cases into four: honorable, discreditable, doubtful, and petty. The doubtful case, which comes the closest to Cicero's ambiguous case, is so because it is partly honorable and partly dishonorable. Obscure cases such as those for which Cicero allows, are not taken into consideration in this categorization.

    118. *Inv.* 1.21.

    119. Schnackenburg, *Epistles*, 53, grasps the exclusivity of the claim made here: "The witnesses in 1 John 1:1–4 are seeking to convey to their addressees a special experience that was unique to themselves. There is not a single word to suggest that the recipients could share the same unique experience."

    120. *Inv.* 1.23.

    121. *Inst.* 4.5.

The alternative is to associate with the schismatics and lose one's association with God (thus emphasizing the illegitimacy of the opponents). Upon what grounds can the author make such a claim? The immediate basis for such a claim is the tradition (μαρτυροῦμεν καὶ ἀπαγγέλλομεν ὑμῖν τὴν ζωὴν τὴν αἰώνιον) of the author. But the crucial question is, "What is the basis for the author's tradition?" It is this question that scholarship seeks to answer when offering various explanations for the language of sensory perception in vv. 1 and 2. In evaluating these proposals, it must be recalled that the two sides in a schism are attempting to justify their own position while undercutting that of their opponents. Such a move is accomplished by appealing to means of legitimacy that are inaccessible to the opponents. To appeal to means of legitimacy to which one's opponent has equal access is to undercut one's own position by allowing that the opponent has just as great a claim upon that means of legitimation. It is, in one sense, fighting to a draw since one does not thereby cast oneself as less legitimate as the opponent. However, to allow that the opponent in a schismatic situation is every bit as legitimate as oneself, is to commit an egregious rhetorical blunder. In other words, one must take care in these situations to appeal to a means of legitimacy to which one's opponents have no access.[122] It is by this criterion that the various proposals regarding v. 1 must be judged.

Such a standard immediately rules out the existentialist reading of Bultmann and the pseudepigraphical reading of Strecker. Bultmann's proposal of a nebulous eschatological reality, the experience of which can be described in terms of sensory perception, must be rejected. Such a reading serves a certain hermeneutical purpose by making an ancient text applicable to a modern reader. However, as an historical reconstruction, it offers no scenario by which such an experience would be restricted to the author and those whom he is trying to persuade, and excluding the schismatics from the experience to which he refers would have been a primary goal of the epistolary author. Strecker's hypothesis is even less workable and for a

---

122. It is important once again to stress that the importance of legitimating institutions has very much to do with the perspective of the person or group attempting to access these institutions. The fact that one faction in a schism attempts to appropriate a means of legitimation and views such a means as significant to the discussion does not necessarily mean that the other faction would hold the same opinion and attempt the same appropriation. The implication of this for the present discussion is that it cannot be inferred from the author's appeal to eye-witness testimony that the opponents would place an equal value on eye-witness testimony. In this Schnackenburg is correct: the author appeals to eye-witness testimony as a means of legitimating his position because he is eager to undercut what he perceives as the opponents' rejection of the incarnation.

greater number of reasons. Strecker's overall reconstruction of the situation behind the composition of the Letters is so different than the one I have accepted here that the two are hardly comparable. His proposal regarding pseudepigraphy then becomes wholly unworkable when brought over into the historical scenario as I have reconstructed it. It is entirely implausible that the epistolary author should compose a letter meant to directly address the schism and attribute the letter to someone who is deceased. Schnackenburg's proposal has more merit, but still fails to convince. He is surely correct when he argues that 1:1-4 are meant to contradict the opponents. However, his rationale seems to be motivated by a desire to take seriously the language of this pericope while maintaining that an eye-witness did not pen it. The result is his somewhat paradoxical conclusion that the author uses the language of history to describe an historical event all the while maintaining that the author's concerns are not historical. What then of the proposals of Brown and Painter?

I first ought to note that these two proposals are not radically different from one another. While Brown argues that a literary convention of the time is being employed and Painter sees the language as theologically colored, both are arguing that the language of sensory perception is being employed by the epistolary author in order to strengthen his connection to the historical tradition-bearers of the community, who were indeed eye-witnesses. The form may be different, but the function is quite the same. These proposals may at first seem to be excluded by my argument concerning appropriating means of legitimation. Could not the opponents just as easily lay claim to the community's tradition-bearers as does the author? However, what I have argued concerning the heterogeneity of the group may allow for the possibility of either of these two proposals being correct. If the community was a heterogeneous one in which ethnic and perhaps economic differences caused a stratification that excluded newcomer Gentiles from places of status and authority within the community, then the author's appeal to access to the tradition of the community may indeed be one that excludes the opponents from making the same claim. But what of the position that the author is indeed laying claim to his own status as an eye-witness?

From the standpoint of laying exclusive claim to a legitimating institution, the eye-witness theory is the strongest. If the author was indeed an eye-witness to the ministry of the historical Jesus, then he is making a claim that his opponents cannot match. The epistolary author is able to conclusively refute the Christological progressivism of the schismatics because he not only saw and heard Jesus, but touched him with his own hands. It would be, in a very real sense, the ultimate rhetorical and strategic move. He lays claim to a status within the group that is exclusively his. In a very real sense, he is not laying claim to the community's tradition; he actually embodies the community's tradition.

Can a case be made for either proposal? Actual eye-witness testimony would be the ultimate claim to legitimacy in this particular schismatic situation. On the other hand, if the community were in fact stratified, then the author may indeed be able to appeal to the community's tradition in such a way that the schismatics are excluded from making a similar claim. In addition, Brown's and Painter's proposals would allow for the death of the Beloved Disciple. As noted above, the death of a movement's charismatic leader can often usher in a period of volatility in the life of the movement, thus precipitating schism. If this were the case with the Johannine Epistles, then we may have one more factor contributing to the breakup of the community. Absent the leadership of the Beloved Disciple, the community begins to fragment as the newcomer Gentiles attempt to reformulate the community's Christological tradition and the old guard opposes them. The late dating of the Epistles work against the eye-witness reading, but Kruse's critique of Brown's proposal demonstrates rather clearly that Brown has overstated his case, even if Kruse has not so thoroughly refuted Brown as he believes.

What may tip the scales in favor of direct eye-witness testimony is the fact that the author establishes his own character and authority by appealing to eyewitness testimony and then does not return to the subject. It is noteworthy that the author attacks the schismatics as diabolical and antichrists and argues that they are "progressive" (applying contemporary labels such as "progressive" to a group of ancient Mediterraneans runs the risk of anachronism, but this particular label seems to be well-suited to the situation given the epistolary author's description of the schismatics in 2 John 9 as πᾶς ὁ προάγων καὶ μὴ μένων ἐν τῇ διδαχῇ τοῦ Χριστοῦ; in the mind of the epistolary author, and in the minds of most ancient Mediterranean people generally, such movement beyond the bounds of accepted tradition would have been quite negative), but never attacks them as illegitimately laying claim to a tradition to which they have no right. Instead, he seems to contrast himself with them in 1:1-4 by stating that he has seen with his eyes and handled with his hands that to which he bears witness. The schismatics, by implication, have not.

A final conclusion is not possible here given the limited amount of data that is available. What may be said is that 1 John 1:1 is not an existential, theological, or literary innovation. Whether directly or indirectly, the epistolary author is appealing to eye-witness testimony as a means of legitimating his own position. This eye-witness testimony is inaccessible to the opponents, and so the author delegitimizes them by appealing to it.

The argument for legitimacy arises again over the issue of the presence of the Spirit in the prophetic activity of each of the factions in the schism. The Spirit[123] is mentioned sparingly in 1 John,[124] but the most expansive of these mentions may provide further insight into the epistolary author's attempt to legitimize himself and his followers while delegitimizing his opponents. 1 John's most extensive remarks on the Spirit come in 3:24—4:3. However, the full context must be taken into account if these four verses are to be fully understood. For this reason, I will include 4:4-6 in the present discussion.[125] 3:24 is not a part of the rhetorical unit that begins with 4:1. It is, in fact, the close of the previous rhetorical unit, which begins in 3:19. However, it does serve to connect the two units by raising the issue of the Spirit and will therefore be included in the discussion.[126]

---

123. There is debate over the exact meaning of πνεῦμα in 1 John. It is clear that the author believes that the πνεῦμα that he possesses is distinct from the πνεῦμα that his opponents possess. I hesitate to risk the anachronism that the capitalization of "Spirit" might imply, but think that it is worth the risk in light of the developed pneumatology that we find in John's Gospel, especially in the farewell discourse.

124. I will here limit the discussion of the Spirit to those passages that refer to πνεῦμα and exclude those referring to χρίσμα and σπέρμα. For a cogent discussion of these terms in relation to the Spirit in 1 John, see Burge, *The Anointed Community*, 174-78.

125. The exact terminus for this rhetorical/literary unit is difficult to determine and there is disagreement in the literature on this point. Schnackenburg, *Epistles*, pp. 198ff., delimits the unit as 4:1-6, as does Brown, *Epistles*, 485ff. Yarbrough, *1-3 John*, 219-30, divides the pericope in two, treating 1-3 and 4-6 as separate units. Moberly, "'Test the Spirits'" 301-5, decries the fact that such divisions are made and treats the entire chapter as a rhetorical unit. Regardless of the overall rhetorical structure and the delimitations thereof, I will treat 1-6 together given that these passages seem to best articulate the epistolary author's views of the Spirit and the effects of the Spirit in the life of the true believer.

126. The overlap between the two units that we find in 3:24 may in fact be quite strong, thus making 3:24 just as much as part of what follows as what precedes. This impression is strengthened when we note that 3:24 seems to form an inclusio with 4:6 signaled by ἐν τούτῳ γινώσκομεν in the former and ἐκ τούτου γινώσκομεν in the latter.

When compared to the claim to eyewitness testimony in 1:1–4, the appeal to the Spirit exhibits some striking parallels as well as divergences. 4:6, with its claim that ἡμεῖς ἐκ τοῦ θεοῦ ἐσμεν· ὁ γινώσκων τὸν θεὸν ἀκούει ἡμῶν, ὃς οὐκ ἔστιν ἐκ τοῦ θεοῦ οὐκ ἀκούει ἡμῶν sounds very much like 1:3 with its highly exclusive claims regarding the necessity of the recipients' fellowship with the sender(s) in order for them to have fellowship with God. The test of the Spirit then is much like the acceptance or rejection of the testimony of the author: If one rejects it, one also rejects God. If one accepts it, one also accepts God. The opponents, however, are much more prominent in this passage than in 1:1–4. 4:3 states: καὶ πᾶν πνεῦμα ὃ μὴ ὁμολογεῖ τὸν Ἰησοῦν ἐκ τοῦ θεοῦ οὐκ ἔστιν· καὶ τοῦτό ἐστιν τὸ τοῦ ἀντιχρίστου. What is particularly striking about this passage is its use of τοῦ ἀντιχρίστου to modify the spirit that does not confess rightly. 1 John 2:18–19 quite explicitly connects the concept of the eschatological antichrist figure (whom I shall discuss below) with the schismatics. Both the fact that the schismatics left, abandoning the community's Christological tradition, and the fact that their spirit confesses wrongly indicate that they are antichrists and not to be believed, trusted, or followed. By presenting his argument this way, the epistolary author has raised the stakes, just as in 1:1–4, but has also brought the schismatics into the conversation in an overt manner.

The meat of the argument is that a distinction should be made between the *Spirit* possessed by the epistolary author and his followers and the *spirit* possessed by the schismatics. The crucial issue seems to be that little distinction can be made between the epistolary author and the opponents in this particular matter. The opponents seem to claim the same Spirit of inspiration as does the epistolary author. The opponents seem to practice their prophetic gift in the same way as the epistolary author. The only difference to which the epistolary author can point is the end result of this prophetic activity, the confession made by the inspired prophet. It is this point that the author attacks.

Not every spirit can be trusted, says the author, because "many false prophets have gone out into the world." (4:1, my translation) This is one instance where the mirror-reading strategy mentioned above might be profitably and safely employed.[127] The issue of the confession that the prophet makes by means of the spirit that inspires him or her arises rather abruptly

---

127. My mirror-reading here will be limited to the actual practice of prophecy with the Johannine community. The epistolary author claims that the schismatics μὴ ὁμολογεῖ τὸν Ἰησοῦν ἐκ τοῦ θεοῦ. Unfortunately, mirror-reading cannot reveal to us the true content of the schismatics' confession, for reasons given above.

and is not accompanied by any proofs that such an event has occurred or is occurring. The impression that one gets is that the epistolary author expects the readers/hearers to be familiar with the situation to which he is referring and to agree with his basic evaluation. The use of "antichrist" to further define them associates them with the schismatics. The schismatics claim to be, in the evaluation of the epistolary author, spirit-inspired prophets, or at least some of them do so. I see no reason to dispute this assertion. My primary rationale is the point of attack that the epistolary author assumes when polemicizing against their spirit-inspired "confessions" (πᾶν πνεῦμα ὃ μὴ *ὁμολογεῖ*; emphasis mine). The epistolary author does not question the validity of the prophetic office or function, nor does he criticize any particular prophetic practices of the schismatics. Rather, he disputes that they are inspired by the Spirit of Truth, which is from God. Thus, in the epistolary author's view, the only distinction that can be made between himself and his opponents in this matter is the substance of their confession. The impression one gets in reading this polemic is that the author cannot discern any difference in the way that prophecy is practiced by both factions. One can very well imagine that a situation has arisen in which the two factions within the community share a common prophetic practice that is resulting in different prophetic utterances, thereby helping to fuel the schism.

The argument for legitimacy by the epistolary author falls into several distinct categories. The issue of the Spirit of Truth and the Spirit's activity within the community comes up several times in 1 John and indicates, I believe, that the author views the opponents as claiming inspiration from the Spirit as legitimation for their own theological claims. These claims by the opponents cannot be left unaddressed, but must be attacked and undercut because possession of the Spirit indicates not only access to God but also God's approval. If the opponents truly possess the Spirit then their position is legitimate and that of the author is not. If the Spirit is such a strong legitimating factor and the differing confessions of the two parties must exclude one or the other from truly possessing the Spirit, then the author must demonstrate that he and his allies are the true possessors of the Spirit and the opponents are not. However, he cannot deny the validity of their experience so he must attack the origins of the Spirit which the opponents possess. Thus the origin of the Spirit can only be determined by the content of the confession offered by those who claim to possess the Spirit, and so the fact that the confession of the opponents is, according to the author, false proves that the Spirit which they possess is not from God.

The dualistic worldview of the author then necessitates that any Spirit that is not from God must be from the Devil. Contrarily, the confession of the author and his allies is true and correct, therefore their Spirit is from God.

As such, the author indicates that he views truth in both monolithic and dualistic terms; the truth itself is a single, unified whole and confession of the truth should reflect this. Thus there is no room for differing perspectives on the truth. Further, what is not truth must be falsehood. Therefore, if the opponents confess something other than the traditional confession of the author and his community, then they must have fallen into error and falsehood. By framing the argument in these terms, the author attempts to legitimize his group by affirming their rightful claim to the Spirit while undercutting the legitimacy of the opponents by asserting that their spirit is diabolical.

Unable to critique the schismatics' prophetic practice, the epistolary author attacks the result of the prophetic practice, that is, the prophetic utterances offered by the schismatics. 1 John 4:1 frames the appeal to legitimacy as an exhortation to test the various prophetic spirits that are in operation. This test is necessitated because many false prophets exist and they are associated with the world, that is, with sin, darkness, falsehood, and separation from God. The Spirit of Truth is evidenced by agreement with the tradition of the community that Jesus Christ has come in the flesh. The spirit that confesses Jesus is not from God (the negatively stated statement is the epistolary author's formulation: πᾶν πνεῦμα ὃ μὴ ὁμολογεῖ τὸν Ἰησοῦν ἐκ τοῦ θεοῦ οὐκ ἔστιν) and is in fact the spirit of antichrist. Verses 4–6 doubly damn the schismatics. Not only does their false spirit and prophecy associate them with the antichrist, but it also firmly places them in the realm of the world. They are from the world (αὐτοὶ ἐκ τοῦ κόσμου εἰσίν), they speak from the world, and the world hears their false prophecies. But the epistolary author's readers/hearers are from God and so do not listen to the schismatics, but listen to the author. One might expect the author to have said that the hearers/readers hear God because they are from God. However, the epistolary author's claim is that fellowship with God and fellowship with the epistolary author himself are inseparable.

The Victimized Community

In conjunction with the community's appeal to the Spirit and the author's eyewitness testimony as evidence of the truth of its claim, the author both accuses the opponents of witchcraft and casts the community as being the victims of the opponents' aggression as a means of establishing the community's righteousness and the opponents' wickedness. I will begin the discussion with the witchcraft accusations and proceed to the author's casting of his followers as victims of the schismatics' aggression.

The terms "witch," "witchcraft," and "witchcraft accusation" are drawn from the field of cultural anthropology and are used as heuristic tools, helping to both identify and describe certain cultural phenomena that occur in particular societies, including the ancient Mediterranean world. As such, these terms reflect, in part, the needs and concerns of the investigator/interpreter and may not necessarily be used by the groups themselves to describe the situations and persons in question. Thus, a social-scientific approach to interpretation might label an exchange in a text as involving a witchcraft accusation when none of the terminology is found in the text. The evidence for a witchcraft accusation, then, is not to be found in these specific terms, but in the process of accusation, the nature of the accusation, and the purpose of the accusation.

"Witch" itself is defined as a person who is able to cause others misfortune through a special propensity (voluntary or involuntary) toward evil.[128] The witchcraft accusation itself has been defined by Mary Douglas having three elements: (1) describing the "witch" as internally corrupt; (2) the "witch" is described as having a perverted inner nature, but this inner nature is covered by an outward veneer of social respectability; and (3) the "witch" is accused of operating by means of "life-sucking" or poisoning.[129] The function of the witchcraft accusation is essentially to eradicate deviant behavior within a group.[130] When a member or group of members begins to behave in a manner that is incompatible with the group's norms, one means of social pressure available to the larger group is the witchcraft accusation. If this social pressure is not effective in bringing the member or group of members back into conformity with the larger group's standards, the accused are expelled from the group or the accusers themselves withdraw from the group, refusing to be polluted by the accused.[131]

---

128. Murdock, *Theories of Illness: A World Survey*, 21.

129. "Introduction," xxvi–xxvii; and *Natural Symbols*, 113.

130. Douglas, "Introduction," xviii; and *Natural Symbols*, 114. See also Mair, *Witchcraft*, 203, 216.

131. Ibid., 114.

When discussing witchcraft and witchcraft accusations in relation to early Christianity and early Christian texts a few additional observations should be made. First, it is a commonplace in social-scientific interpretation of the New Testament that ancient Mediterranean peoples were essentially dyadic rather than individualistic. Therefore, the focus in evaluating character was placed on external and often stereotypical traits. Where was one from? To what family did one belong? What was one's ethnicity? However, there still seems to have been a recognition among ancient Mediterraneans that humans did indeed have an interior existence that might not square with external appearance.[132] This recognition created tension and fear that a group could be invaded by someone who was not what he or she seemed to be. This tension between external appearance and internal reality plays into the first and second points made by Douglas regarding witchcraft accusations. Secondly, simple duplicity was not enough to constitute a witch; the duplicity must be accompanied by a supernatural empowerment to inflict harm, and this power was provided, in the minds of the New Testament writers, usually by demons but sometimes by the Devil himself. For instance, the eschatological opponent in Rev 13, the beast from the sea, is empowered by the Dragon (Satan) to rule over the nations, leading Malina and Pilch to characterize the beast as the Dragon's "vice-regent,"[133] and Matthew 12:24 depicts the Pharisees accusing Jesus of conducting exorcisms by the power of Beelzebul.[134] The exchange between Jesus and "the Jews" in John 8:48–49 is a good example of associating deviants with the demonic. The third additional point to be made is that these two aspects of witchcraft accusations, tension between external and internal and diabolical empowerment, are often combined in New Testament texts. So, for example, we will have groups labeled as both hypocrites and having a demon or demons.[135]

132. Malina and Neyrey, *Calling Jesus Names*, 17.

133. *Social-Science Commentary on the Book of Revelation*, 170. It is worth noting that the idea of vice-regency fits in with one of the possible uses of αντι. See above.

134. As Malina and Neyrey point out, New Testament texts tend to associate witchcraft accusations with acts of healing or exorcism, and the means by which these miracles are effected, it is argued, are diabolical. Witchcraft accusations are found in the Gospel of John (8:44, 48), though they here are not directly linked to any particular sign performed by Jesus, being rather embedded in the middle of a lengthy discourse. Malina and Rohrbaugh, *Social-Science Commentary on the Gospel of John*, 160–67, do not discuss witchcraft accusations in reference to this pericope, but Neyrey, *The Gospel of John*, 162–63, does regard it as such.

135. For examples from the Gospel of Matthew and further discussion, see Malina and Neyrey, *Calling Jesus Names*, 26, 64–66.

Applying the Model

Having said something of the nature of witchcraft accusations, let us move on to an examination of the witchcraft accusations in the Epistles.

2 John 1:8 provides the reader with a startling caution: βλέπετε ἑαυτούς, ἵνα μὴ ἀπολέσητε ἃ εἰργασάμεθα ἀλλὰ μισθὸν πλήρη ἀπολάβητε. The schism has placed the addressees in danger of losing that for which they have worked. But how has this danger arisen? I will argue that the danger is present in the form of "witches," the schismatics, who are able to "poison" the epistolary author's addressees through their deceitful teaching. Part of the epistolary author's rhetorical aim, then, is to identify the "witches" as such so that the community can remove them and so rid themselves of the danger.

Neyrey argues that 5 passages in 1 and 2 John can be classified as witchcraft accusations, and I will consider them here.[136] Three themes tend to repeat in these five passages: the schismatics are identified with the eschatological opponent, the antichrist, of the community's tradition; the schismatics are cast as deceivers (πλάνοι); and they are said to be "of the Devil" (ἐκ τοῦ διαβόλου). Strikingly, there is such overlap between the various labels that the reader begins to get the impression that they are almost synonymous in the eyes of the epistolary author.

The first accusation, that the schismatics are antichrists, can be found in 1 John 2:18, 22; 4:3; and 2 John 7. Specifically, this accusation is tied to denial that Jesus Christ has come in the flesh (4:2, 3; 2 John 7) and it represents a modification of the community's eschatological tradition. The epistolary author opens this element of the accusation in dramatic style by claiming that the appearance of the schismatics signals ἐσχάτη ὥρα.[137]

---

136. *Gospel of John*, 163. They are 1 John 2:18, 22; 3:8-10; 4:1-3; 2 John 7.

137. The anarthrous nature of the phrase is virtually universally understood as unimportant by commentators. It should be understood as "*the* last hour." The exact nature of this last hour, however, is the subject of a bit more debate. A minority of commentators argue for various understandings of the phrase that avoid the embarrassment of admitting that the epistolary author was incorrect in so strenuously arguing that the final hour had come. Marshall, *Epistles*, 149-50, follows Bruce in arguing that "the last hour" is a period of time that can extend indefinitely, running parallel with the passage of time. Smalley, *1, 2, 3 John, Revised*, 92, argues that ὥρα can be a brief moment in time or an extended period, thus allowing the ambiguity of the term to rescue the epistolary author. Witherington III, *Letters and Homilies*, 483-84, argues that the whole of the period between Pentecost and the parousia is in mind. The majority of commentators, however, opt for understanding the epistolary author quite literally: the appearance of the schismatics indicates that the parousia is imminent. See Brown, *Epistles*, 330-32; Dodd, *Epistles*, 51; Kruse, *Letters*, 98; Lieu, *I, II, III John*, 98-99; Painter, *1, 2, and 3 John*, 197; Strecker, *Letters*, 62.

The author imagines the schism as ushering in a moment of eschatological significance and this moment may indeed have been the return of Christ. The community's tradition seems to have taught that this moment begins with the appearance of antichrist, whom the community has heard is coming. But the epistolary author reinterprets the community's tradition so that the schismatics themselves become a plurality of antichrists.[138] While there is no explicit connection in the Epistles between antichrist and the Devil/Satan, it might be reasonably inferred that such a connection did exist.

Drawing directly from the epistolary texts themselves, it might be noted that the αντι prefix that is attached to χρίστος is generally taken to signify replacement, but most commentators here take it primarily in the sense of opposition.[139] The temporal context for the depiction is eschatological, given that the epistolary author sees the advent of the schismatic antichrists as signaling the last hour. We therefore have a figure who sets himself[140] up in opposition to God and God's Christ in an eschatological context. Given these two basic facts, we are able to infer that 1 John 2:18; 4:3; and 2 John 7 probably have in mind ideas similar to those found in other texts that depict an eschatological figure who is opposed to God and/or God's messiah.[141]

Revelation 13's beast from the sea, mentioned above, is a ready example of the eschatological opponent who is closely associated with the Devil. In vv. 1, 5, and 6, the beast's opposition to God is illustrated through

---

138. It is worth noting that the schism seems to have occurred because the schismatics had engaged in reinterpreting the community's christological tradition, but the epistolary author seems comfortable in reinterpreting the community's *antichristological* tradition.

139. See Brown, *Epistles*, 333. Brown also notes that ἀντι can be used in the sense of an illegitimate replacement. In that case, he sees a possible parallel to the idea of ψευδοχριστοι in Matt 24:24 and Mark 13:32. Indeed, it seems quite possible that nuances of all three meanings are intended in its usage here. An argument that is interestingly lacking in the literature is that ἀντι does here have the sense of replacement. In this case, the epistolary author could be referring to the fact that the schismatics have replaced the Christ of the Johannine tradition with a new Christ that is no Christ at all, a pseudochrist who is opposed to the true.

140. The eschatological opponent of the biblical and intertestamental literature is depicted as male, when human.

141. Brown's discussion of the background of the antichrist figure in *Epistles*, 333–36, is succinct, yet helpful in that it compresses a great deal of information into a brief summary. His categories of (1) the satan, (2) the sea monster, (3) the human ruler embodying evil, and (4) the false prophet are helpful and will be appropriated here. See also Bousset's classic study, *The Antichrist Legend*.

his blasphemous speech, and v. 7 depicts the beast as making war on God's saints. In v. 4 we find that this beast who is opposed to God, uttering blasphemies, is given authority by the Dragon, the Devil. Similarly, 2 Thess 2:7-12 speaks of the mystery of lawlessness (τὸ μυστήριον τῆς ἀνομίας; it is worth noting that 1 John 3:4 equates lawlessness with sin) and its future revelation, at which time the lawless one will come and will be empowered by Satan (κατ' ἐνέργειαν τοῦ σατανᾶ) to work "lying wonders" (τέρασιν ψεύδους).

Similarly, 1 John 3:8–10 connects sin and hatred of the brothers and sisters with the Devil and being of the Devil (ἐκ τοῦ διαβόλου). These references are located in the larger rhetorical unit made up of 2:28—3:10.[142] The unit opens by exhorting the hearers/readers to abide in Christ so that they may be confident rather than ashamed when Christ is revealed (φανερωθῇ). The author then immediately takes up a line of argumentation in which he demonstrates that those who behave righteously (πᾶς ὁ μὴ ποιῶν δικαιοσύνην) are children of the righteous God. The unit closes by arguing that the children of God are revealed (ἐν τούτῳ φανερά ἐστιν τὰ τέκνα τοῦ θεοῦ) by their actions. This criterion is summed up in a synonymous parallelism in which the author asserts that those who do not act justly do not belong to God, nor do those who do not love their brothers and sisters. Brown is surely correct when he argues that we do not have here two criteria, but one.[143] Telling is the fact that the author clarifies "those who do not act righteously" by saying that these are the ones who do not love the brothers and sisters (ὁ μὴ ἀγαπῶν τὸν ἀδελφὸν αὐτοῦ). The Epistles do not employ this terminology in a general or vague way. On the contrary, the use of ἀδελφός in the Epistles is to be taken as referring to fellow members of the Johannine community.[144] In addition, the author repeatedly casts his address in intimate tones, addressing the hearers/readers with his characteristic "little children" and making use of fist person plurals when addressing them. The tone is well suited to a polemical context in which the "we" of the epistolary author and his followers stands in contrast to the "them" of the schismatics. The net result is that the author, in describing those who are "of God" and those who are "of the devil", is actually drawing a contrast between himself and his followers on the one hand and the schismatics on the other. By associating the schismatics with the Devil,

---

142. I here use the divisions proposed by Brown, *Epistles*, 378–417.

143. *Epistles*, 417.

144. See Schnackenburg, *Epistles*, 110–14, and Brown, *Epistles*, 269–73.

the epistolary author is able to reveal the true source of the danger in which the community members have been placed: the Devil, working through the schismatics.

But how does the Devil work through the schismatics, and how does this working place the community in danger? The figure of the eschatological opponent is, again, a good starting point. 2 Thess 2:9 speaks of the "lying wonders" performed by the Man of Lawlessness, and this reference serves as a ready example of the association of the eschatological opponent with deceit, a stereotypical characteristic of witches and a characteristic of the schismatics. The depiction of the eschatological opponent as a deceiver is quite consistent. Daniel 11:23 depicts Antiochus IV Epiphanes as deceitful (ποιήσει ψεῦδος). Matthew 24:24, mentioned above, warns against false prophets and false messiahs who will come and lead many astray. The depiction of the eschatological opponent as a deceiver is common enough that Meeks is able to say: "Common to *all* the apocalyptic traditions of the false prophet attested in the New Testament are (I) that he will 'lead astray' the nation(s) . . . ." (emphasis mine).[145] The connection between witchcraft accusations and 1 John are readily observable.

The schismatics, like the eschatological opponent, are depicted as attempting to deceive, to "poison" the innocent. 1 John 2:22 identifies the one who denies that Jesus is the Christ as antichrist, but it also identifies the one who denies as a liar (ψεύστης). 1 John 4:1 connects the spirit that is not from God with the "false prophets" (ψευδοπροφῆται) who have gone out into the world, i.e., the schismatics. 2 John 2:7 makes the connection even more explicit; the antichrists are identified as πλάνοι, the deceivers. The author's concern that the readers should not be deceived by the schismatics extends even beyond those passages formally identified by Neyrey as witchcraft accusations. There are repeated warnings to the hearers/readers to guard against deception. In 1 John 3:7, embedded in the rhetorical unit in which we find the schismatics depicted as of the devil, we also find a warning against deception: Τεκνία, μηδεὶς πλανάτω ὑμᾶς. Similar warnings against deception can be found in 1:8 and 2:26. The epistolary author also argues that those who make certain claims or engage in certain actions are themselves liars or would presume to make God a liar (1:10; 2:4; 4:20; 5:10). In this way, the epistolary author stresses that the basic characteristic of a witch, deceitfulness, is to be found in the schismatics.

---

145. *The Prophet-King*, 49.

Applying the Model

But despite their best efforts, the schismatics cannot disguise their true nature. Their actions expose them: ἐν τούτῳ φανερά ἐστιν τὰ τέκνα τοῦ θεοῦ καὶ τὰ τέκνα τοῦ διαβόλου, 1 John 3:10. The point of the author exposing the schismatics' true nature is to provide the basis and motivation for full separation from them. They have already gone out, but the epistolary author is anxious that none of his followers should waver and follow after them, so he repeatedly affirms their diabolical nature and the dire consequences of believing their lies. These affirmations also have the effect of solidifying group identity; those who have committed to the epistolary author find reassurance that they have made the right decision.

The sum of the matter is that the epistolary author employs witchcraft accusations against the schismatics in two different forms. He implicitly casts them as witches by labeling them as antichrists. In doing so, he brings to the minds of the hearers/readers the traditional concept of the eschatological opponent as a diabolically empowered deceiver and "demythologizes" this tradition by applying it to the flesh and blood schismatics. These schismatics, the epistolary author argues, are empowered by Satan to deceive other members of the community and their activity is helping to usher in the eschaton. He more explicitly labels them as witches when he directly accuses them of deceit and having diabolic origins. He concludes his accusation by pronouncing the unmasking of the schismatics' hypocrisy. They have tried to disguise themselves as true brothers and sisters, but their actions have made it plain that they are children of the Devil. Such exposure, the epistolary author hopes, will serve as a caution to those who might be wavering in their loyalties and further solidify those who have committed themselves to him.

A final example of the epistolary author's attempt to portray the schismatics as illegitimate can be found in 1 John 3:11–12. Here the epistolary author reminds the hearers/readers of the proclamation that they had heard from the beginning, that they should love one another. This proclamation is then immediately contrasted with the behavior of Cain, whom the epistolary author depicts as having "butchered" his brother Abel. This behavior is attributed to (1) his descent from the evil one (ἐκ τοῦ πονηροῦ ἦν), and (2) the evil nature of his own deeds (ὅτι τὰ ἔργα αὐτοῦ πονηρὰ ἦν). The argumentation here is highly negative and serves the negative purpose of undermining the credibility of the schismatics, but it must be remembered that the epistolary author's ultimate goal is positive: the negative example of Cain is brought up in order to encourage in the hearers/readers the positive characteristic of love for one's neighbor.[146] That being said, the negative argumentation does provide the epistolary author with another opportunity to excoriate the schismatics.

The schismatics are not mentioned directly in these two verses, but their presence is readily apparent. The opening exhortation to the hearers/readers is that they should love one another. This reminder is necessary because of the schismatics' display of an apparent lack of love for the other community members in rending the community. But the inference becomes even clearer in the choice of illustration. The fact that Cain and Abel are brothers plays into the community's own terminology quite well. The schismatics fit the profile of Cain and the epistolary author and his followers are cast as righteous and victimized Abel. The betrayal of group loyalty that occurs in the schism is, in the eyes of the epistolary author, nothing short of a brutally violent murder.

It is neither accidental nor unimportant that the epistolary author uses such violent imagery and language in describing the behavior of the schismatics. Σφάζειν literally means "to butcher," and is often used in cultic contexts in LXX (cf. LXX Lev. 4:4, 15; and 6:18 as brief examples; there are, by my count, 40 uses of this verb in Lev.), though it does not have any inherently cultic connotations. It occurs quite often in Revelation, which uses it to describe the lamb who was "slain" (Rev 5:6, 9, 12; 13:8), the violence of warfare (6:4), the martyrs (6:9, and, perhaps, 18:24), and the wounding unto death of one of the heads of the dragon (13:8), thus displaying the variety of contexts in which this term can be used. The real impact of the verb comes not from the context that it connotes, but the violence that it depicts, thus my rendering of it as "to butcher." The epistolary author goes beyond the Genesis account, which simply uses ἀποκτείνω to describe Cain's action against Abel. This change in vocabulary serves to emphasize the violence and savagery of the act. Such an emphasis is not for mere shock value; ancient Mediterranean cultures tended to hold specific attitudes regarding the appropriateness of the use of physical violence in personal conflicts.

Several options for resolving an honor/shame exchange were available to ancient Mediterranean peoples and groups, and Malina and Rohrbaugh discuss one of these options: one of the two parties resorts to violence in order to resolve the dispute.[147] Honor challenges could reach the point

---

146. See Brown, *Epistles*, 468–69; Witherington III, *Letters and Homilies*, 507–8; and Yarbrough, *1–3 John*, 197.

147. *John*, 191.

Applying the Model

at which one side felt that its honor had been so badly damaged by the exchange that a violent retaliation was necessary and justified. However, the resort to violence often led to further retaliation by the other party and the situation could rapidly devolve into a blood feud, so a high priority tended to be placed on keeping violence curtailed in these honor challenges. Nevertheless, in dire circumstances, such an approach could be viewed as a legitimate way to maintain one's honor. On the other hand, a hasty resort to violence demonstrated the dishonorable nature of the party taking such actions. The abandonment of verbal sparring for physical sparring was a sign of that party's inability to defend its honor.

> In a sense, then, the overquick resort to violence in a challenge-response situation was not only dangerous, it was frequently an unintended public admission of failure in the game of wits. The death of a challenger was sometimes a worthy response to public dishonor, but an overquick resort to violence was an inadvertent admission that one had lost control of the challenge situation. Wits have failed and bully tactics have taken over.[148]

Cain's assault of Abel would seem to fit quite well with this scenario. Cain's violent response to God's preference of Abel's gift is depicted in the Genesis story as thoroughly dishonorable. The epistolary author's appropriation of the story in describing the interactions between his party and the schismatics does not mean that physical violence had actually erupted within the community. The probability is actually that it had not, given that the epistolary author resorts to the use of Old Testament imagery rather than concrete examples from the community's history in formulating his argument. Rather, the epistolary author takes this opportunity to paint the schism itself, the act of separation, as an act of violence against the community. Rather than continue the engagement in an honorable manner, matching wits against one another, the schismatics have taken the dishonorable approach of withdrawing themselves, tearing the community apart. Such discrediting serves to solidify group identity and cohesion in that it confirms to the faithful that they have made the right decision. They have sided with the epistolary author and their side is righteous. They have behaved

---

148. Ibid. Their comments are made regarding John 10:32, in which "the Jews" confront Jesus in Solomon's Stoa, demanding that he tell them whether or not he claims to be the Messiah. The exchange very quickly comes to the point that the Pharisees attempt to stone Jesus. A similar story is to be found in Luke 4:16–30, in which Jesus claims that Isaiah 61:1–2 has been fulfilled. Those present them lead him out to the edge of a cliff with the intent of throwing him over the edge, though he escapes.

honorably in the course of the schism, as opposed to the dishonorable behavior of the schismatics. For those who are vacillating, hesitant to fully commit to one side or the other, the argument serves to cast the epistolary author and his followers as the correct and honorable side in the dispute.

An added facet of this passage is that, much like the witchcraft accusations mentioned above, the epistolary author connects the violent behavior of the schismatics with the Devil. Cain, the epistolary author claims, was "of the Evil One" (ἐκ τοῦ πονηροῦ ἦν) and that his own deeds were evil (τὰ ἔργα αὐτοῦ πονηρὰ ἦν). Cain's motivation is two-fold: His origins dictate that his behavior will tend toward the evil, but his brother's righteous behavior serves as a contrast to his evil behavior, thereby highlighting the evilness of Cain's behavior. In other words, Abel's righteous behavior exposes Cain's evil behavior and origins for what they are. The "witch" has been uncovered and so he retaliates violently and hastily.

The third and final point to draw from this passage is that the epistolary author depicts himself and his followers as righteous and honorable. The epistolary author was willing to continue the challenge and response sequence in this dispute, and indeed he continues to challenge the schismatics through his epistles. The schismatics, however, did not have the honor to continue the exchange. Instead, they withdrew from the process, thereby exposing their evil and dishonorable nature. In addition, the fact that the epistolary author and his followers have suffered this abuse at the hands of the schismatics only serves to demonstrate that they themselves are righteous and honorable. The depiction is both polemical and persuasive. The followers' own righteousness is affirmed, assuring them that they have made the correct decision in remaining faithful to the community and its teachings, while those who are as of yet undecided should be persuaded to side with the righteous and honorable epistolary author and his followers rather than the evil and dishonorable schismatics.

V

Conclusion

Previous Evaluations of the Problem

THE SCHISM REFLECTED IN 1 and 2 John has been the focus of scholarly inquiry into these epistles for nearly a century now, and much of scholarship during that period argued that a proper understanding of the author and his Epistles cannot be had without a proper reconstruction of the author's opponents. Various reading strategies were then been proposed, and while there is overlap between the proposed reconstructions of the opponents' beliefs, the full spectrum of the reconstructions tends to be rather divergent. Reading strategies include reading the opponents in light of the Gospel, reading the opponents in light of later Patristic literature, and isolating the σπέρμα and χρίσμα passages. The results yielded tend to be equally divergent: the opponents are simply Johannine Christians who have taken some implicit thoughts of the Gospel to their logical conclusions, or they are proto-Gnostics whose thought would later develop into Docetism and the like, or they are a unique Gnostic group otherwise unknown to us. The problem with both the strategies and the reconstructions derived from them is that they implicitly understand 1 and 2 John as accurately reflecting the beliefs of the opponents. Those who would read the Epistles non-polemically rightly point out the fault in this foundational supposition, and my own examination of the rhetoric of religious schism strongly indicates that the goal of such language is not to provide accurate depictions of the opponents' beliefs but to excoriate the opponents so that they lose the support of their followers and/or does not gain any new followers.

On the other hand, the model of religious schism articulated in this study contradicts the non-polemicists' assertion that the schism had little if anything to do with the composition of the Epistles. Indeed, a schism is a trauma that can only be healed over extended periods of time and by much re-visitation of the event and verbal processing.

What is needed is (1) a shift in focus away from the opponents and toward the epistolary author and (2) a methodological framework that is tailored to the schismatic process so that our inquiry is not arbitrary but guided by what can be known about the general process of religious schism.

Constructing a Model

The model requires us to make general inquiries into the nature of the Johannine community, so that we begin with a broad inquiry that takes in the full scope of the Johannine literature, including Revelation. As the model moves into the particulars of religious schism, additional models must be employed, including models of witchcraft and the rules of social conflict in ancient Mediterranean societies.

The model itself begins with a discussion of the motivations for schism, reviewing Niebuhr's work on denominationalism and his proposal that all religious schism was rooted in material concerns. Zuckerman, however, has challenged this theory and has demonstrated in his exhaustive case study of the schism in Temple Am Israel that schism is sometimes caused by ideological differences that have no apparent material motivation. Our inquiry into schism must, therefore, allow for a range of motivating factors; motivation may be found in the material or the ideological, or possibly in a combination of the two.

Once it has been determined that motivation for schism exists, we must also determine a group's propensity to schism. Wallis argues that the propensity to schism depends primarily upon (1) the presence of a charismatic leader and (2) the ability of the leader and the schismatic group to appropriate the parent group's means of legitimation or formulate their own new means of legitimation. Wallis charted the propensity to schism based upon availability of legitimating institutions so that groups which have a single legitimating institution that is available to one person in the group are least likely to experience schism, while those that have many legitimating institutions that are available to all group members are most likely to experience schism.

The likelihood that schism will occur also depends upon the groups' views of themselves as uniquely or pluralistically legitimate. Pluralistically legitimate groups view themselves as legitimate but allow that other groups may be legitimate as well. Uniquely legitimate groups, on the other hand, see themselves as legitimate and deny, to some degree, the legitimacy of other groups. While Wallis presented these two options as an either/or choice, I modified them to represent extremes on a spectrum.

The schismatic process itself begins with the formation of homogeneous cliques within a larger heterogeneous group. The formation of cliques is to be expected in any large group and does not in itself necessitate that a schism will occur. The trouble begins when the clique becomes alienated from the rest of the group. If the alienation of the clique goes unresolved, the clique becomes an exit group that begins to engage in the process of talking itself out of the larger group. Schismatic polemic typically begins within the exit group and is not necessarily overtly directed at the larger group. However, as alienation increases, the polemic rises and both parties become engaged in the exchange. From the perspective of the larger group, the level of polemic is generally an indication of the size and/or importance of the schismatic group. Schismatic groups that are larger and/or have higher social standing within the larger group will elicit a stronger response from the larger group, while groups that are smaller and/or have lower social standing will elicit a less vigorous response. The polemic that is exchanged tends to escalate as the two groups work through the process of separation, and a point may be reached where the polemic is highly vitriolic and dehumanizing. An important aspect of the polemic is that each group will eventually lay absolute claim to legitimacy. At least temporarily and at least in relation to one another, the two groups will become uniquely legitimate. Therefore, each side must depict the other as illegitimate.

The schism itself tends to endure in the collective memory of the two groups, especially the schismatic group, and the issues over which the schism occurred will become central to the identity of the groups, at least for a while. The schismatic group itself may meet with a variety of fates. Further schism is not uncommon, nor is complete dissolution of the group. Some schismatic groups endure, however, and continue to tell the story of the schism.

The Nature of the Community

The result of the application of this model to 1 and 2 John yields a variety of results. The Johannine community is, it would appear, a rather uniquely legitimate group. They view Greco-Roman religion as not simply illegitimate, but diabolical. Any association with the institutions of Greco-Roman religion is association with Satan and cannot be tolerated. Judaism fairs better in the eyes of the Johannine community, but not by much. While the language of diabolical association is toned down, the Gospel of John calls "the Jews" the children of the Devil, and Revelation twice refers to "the synagogue of Satan." While these may be taken as polemical attacks against specific groups within Judaism, Judaism as a whole is understood as passé. The Torah was valid for its time, but the more complete revelation of Jesus Christ has come, fulfilling all that the Torah anticipated. The scriptures and practices of Judaism are beneficial in that they give testimony to Jesus, but Torah observance is no longer necessary. Non-Johannine Christianity is seen as acceptable, but it seems to be viewed as inferior to the Johannine community's tradition and theology. There is evidence that the Johannine community experienced some sort of distance between itself and other Christian groups and that the leadership of the community was attempting to close that distance and possibly join non-Johannine Christianity. However, the fact that appeal needed to be made to close that distance may also indicate that some among the community were resistant to that change. The net result is that we have a group that views non-Christians as illegitimate and other non-Johannine Christians as legitimate but inferior.

The center of the Johannine community was its Christology. It would seem that the community's Christological tradition was the point of dispute in its earlier separation from the synagogue, and this dispute may actually have accelerated the community's move toward a higher Christology. Given that the community's Christology was purchased at so high a price, it also became the point at which the community was most uniquely legitimate and therefore least tolerant of deviance. The premium that the community placed upon its Christology helps in part to explain the apparently vitriolic nature of the ensuing dispute.

The Johannine community is also revealed to be a heterogeneous group that was probably composed of both Jewish and Gentile sub-groups, the Jewish sub-group being the earlier of the two. In addition, the Gentile component may very well have been financially better off than the Jewish group and may also have had a higher standing in society generally. The timing of the Gentiles' entry into the community may also be telling. It may very well be that the schismatics were a group of Gentiles who entered the community en masse. This would mean that the Johannine community may have had Gentiles joining the community prior to the entry of what would become the schismatic group, but these earlier Gentile converts would have

Conclusion

entered the community in smaller numbers and over a longer period of time. Despite the fact that the Gentiles joined the community, they did not assimilate into the community, especially positions of leadership, as fully as they expected.[1] The failure to assimilate resulted in a sense of alienation among these Gentile converts and their clique soon became an exit group in which discussion of displeasure with their place in the group was mingled with a reformulating of the community's traditional Christological confession. The two combined to create a situation in which the exit group effected separation, thus bringing confusion into the community. Some members of the community remained faithful to the epistolary author and the community's tradition, while others vacillated between the two sides, their loyalties divided. With these groups in mind, as well as the now absent schismatics, we turn to the rhetorical aim of the epistolary author.

Rhetorical Aim Within the Setting of Religious Schism

The epistolary author at the very outset goes about attempting to establish his own position as legitimate while at the same time casting his opponents, the schismatics, as illegitimate pretenders. He accomplishes this by establishing his own credentials as an eyewitness to the ministry of the historical Jesus (or by at least laying legitimate claim to the eyewitness testimony of his predecessors in the community), thus implying the inability of the schismatics to make a similar counterclaim. He also refutes the schismatics' claim to have the Spirit and instead asserts that he and his followers are the true possessors of the Spirit, even providing a confessional test to employ to determine whose claim is legitimate. He further attacks the legitimacy of the schismatics by depicting them as witches and unable to honorably engage in the challenge-response process. The schismatics are exposed as witches by the fact that they have attempted to deceive the community and

---

1. I have already noted that this point is complicated somewhat by the fact that the epistolary author depicts the schismatics as having been involved in prophetic activity within the community. However, it is clear that the author sees that activity as illegitimate given its heterodox content. Further, it is difficult to assess the place of this prophetic activity—and thereby the place of the schismatics prior to their departure—within the Johannine community. It may very well be the case that such activity was an assertion by the Gentile schismatic group of their place within the community and that this assertiveness was tolerated rather than endorsed by the Jewish-Christian leadership. Thus, while the schismatics' prophetic activity could be seen as raising questions concerning my conclusions, a little historical imagination easily provides contexts for understanding such activity in a way that strengthens rather than weakens my overall argument.

lead it out of fellowship with God. Like all witches, they have diabolical connections, but the epistolary author intensifies this connection by claiming that the schismatics' very origins are diabolical and that they are in fact the diabolically empowered eschatological enemies that the community's tradition identifies as "antichrist." Further dishonor is heaped upon the schismatics by depicting them as Cain, who reacted violently against his brother. This depiction serves to cast the schismatics as unable to hold their own in the verbal back-and-forth of the ancient Mediterranean challenge-response process. Their hasty resort to the violent act of separation from the community demonstrates their dishonor. But what is the aim of all this?

The Epistles were addressed to whole congregations, but within these congregations were individuals or smaller groups of individuals (cliques) whose loyalties to the author and the community were of varying degrees. Some would be fully committed to the community, others committed but questioning their decision, and some on the verge of leaving the community for the side of the opponents. The rhetoric of the Epistles serves to shore up the boundaries of the community by solidifying commitment to the community and its theology. The sharp rhetoric serves to confirm to those who are fully committed to the community that they have indeed made the correct choice, while the second group's wavering commitment is quelled: they have indeed made the correct choice in opting for the author and his community over against the diabolical opponents. The third and final group would find in the Epistles a stern warning against defection. To abandon the community and its tradition is to place oneself in league with error and the Devil and to stand in opposition to righteousness and God. The rhetoric of the Epistles strengthens group identity and boundaries. There is no room or allowance for vacillation in one's commitment to the community's tradition and the Epistles present the options in starkly dualistic terms in order to discourage a continuation of the sort of defection that had already occurred within the community.

Bibliography

Akin, Daniel L. *1, 2, 3 John.* NAC 38. Nashville: Broadman and Holman, 2001.
Albright, W. F. "Discoveries in Palestine and the Gospel of St John." In *The Background of the New Testament and Its Eschatology,* edited by W. D. Davies and D. Daube, 153–71. Cambridge: Cambridge University Press, 1956.
Apostolic Fathers. Translated by Bart D. Ehrman. 2 vols. LCL. Cambridge, MA: Harvard University Press, 2003.
Appel, Heinrich. *Einleitung in das Neue Testament.* Leipzig, 1922.
Aristotle. *The "Art" of Rhetoric.* Translated by J. H. Freese. LCL. Cambridge, MA: Harvard University Press, 2006.
Ashton, John. *Understanding the Fourth Gospel.* 2nd ed. Oxford: Oxford University Press, 2007.
Aune, David E. *Revelation.* 3 vols. WBC 52. Nashville: Nelson, 1997–1998.
Baer, Hans A. *Recreating Utopia in the Desert: A Sectarian Challenge to Modern Mormonism.* New York: State University of New York: 1988.
Barclay, John M. G. "Mirror-Reading a Polemical Letter: Galatians as a Test Case." In *The Galatians Debate: Contemporary Issues in Rhetorical and Historical Interpretation,* edited by Mark D. Nanos, 367–82. Peabody, MA: Hendrickson, 2002.
Barrett, C. K. *The Gospel according to St. John: An Introduction with Commentary and Notes on the Greek Text.* London: SPCK, 1956.
Barton, Stephen C. "Can We Identify the Gospel Audiences?" In *The Gospels for All Christians: Rethinking the Gospel Audiences,* edited by Richard Bauckham, 147–72. Grand Rapids: Eerdmans, 1998.
———. "Johannine Dualism and Contemporary Pluralism." In *The Gospel of John and Christian Theology,* edited by Richard Bauckham and Carl Mosser, 3–18. Grand Rapids: Eerdmans, 2008.
Bauckham, Richard. "For Whom Were the Gospels Written?" In *The Gospels for All Christians: Rethinking the Gospel Audiences,* edited by Richard Bauckham, 9–48. Grand Rapids: Eerdmans, 1998.
———. *The Testimony of the Beloved Disciple: Narrative, History, and Theology in the Gospel of John.* Grand Rapids: Baker Academic, 2007.
Baumgarten, Albert I. "Reflections on the Groningen Hypothesis." In *Enoch and Qumran Origins: New Light on a Forgotten Connection,* edited by Gabriele Boccaccini, 256–62. Grand Rapids: Eerdmans, 2005.
Beale, G. K. *The Book of Revelation.* NIGTC. Grand Rapids: Eerdmans, 1999.
Beasley-Murray, George R. *John.* 2nd ed. WBC 36. Nashville: Nelson, 1999.

BIBLIOGRAPHY

Bernard, J. H. *A Critical and Exegetical Commentary on the Gospel according to St. John*. 2 vols. ICC. Edinburgh: T. & T. Clark, 1928.

Bieringer, Reimund, Didier Pollefeyt, and Frederique Vandecasteele-Vanneuville. *Anti-Judaism and the Fourth Gospel*. Louisville: Westminster John Knox, 2001.

Black, C. Clifton. "1, 2, & 3 John." In *The New Interpreter's Bible Volume XII*, edited by Leander Keck. Nashville: Abingdon, 1998.

Blenkinsopp, Joseph. *Ezra-Nehemiah: A Commentary*. OTL. Louisville: Westminster John Knox, 1988.

———. "A Jewish Sect of the Persian Period." *Catholic Biblical Quarterly* 52 (1990) 5–20.

Blomberg, Craig L. *The Historical Reliability of John's Gospel: Issues and Commentary*. Downer's Grove, IL: IVP, 2001.

Boccaccini, Gabriele. *Beyond the Essene Hypothesis: The Parting of the Ways between Qumran and Enochic Judaism*. Grand Rapids: Eerdmans, 1998.

Bogart, J. *Orthodox and Heretical Perfectionism in the Johannine Community as Evident in the First Epistle of John*. SBLDS 33. Missoula, MT: Scholars, 1977.

Borgen, Peder. "The Gospel of John and Hellenism: Some Observations." In *Exploring the Gospel of John: In Honor of D. Moody Smith*, edited by R. Alan Culpepper and C. Clifton Black, 98–123. Louisville: Westminster John Knox, 1996.

Boring, M. Eugene. *Revelation*. Interpretation. Lousiville: Westminster John Knox, 1989.

Bousset, Wilhelm. *The Antichrist Legend: A Chapter in Christian and Jewish Folklore*. Translated by A. H. Keane. Introduction by D. Frankfurter. AARTTS 24. Atlanta: Scholars, 1999.

———. *Die Offenbarung Johannis*. KEK. Göttingen: Vandenhoek und Ruprecht, 1906.

Boxall, Ian. *The Revelation of Saint John*. BNTC 19. Peabody, MA: Hendrickson, 2006.

Boyarin, Daniel. *Border Lines: The Partition of Judeo-Christianity*. Philadelphia: University of Pennsylvania Press, 2004.

Brooke, A. E. *The Johannine Epistles*. International Critical Commentary. Edinburgh: T. & T. Clark, 1912.

Brown, Raymond E. *The Birth of the Messiah: A Commentary on the Infancy Narratives in the Gospels of Matthew and Luke*. Rev. ed. ABRL. New York: Doubleday, 1993.

———. *The Community of the Beloved Disciple*. New York: Paulist, 1979.

———. *The Death of the Messiah, From Gethsemane to the Grave: A Commentary on the Passion Narratives in the Four Gospels*. 2 vols. ABRL. New York: Doubleday, 1994.

———. *The Epistles of John: A New Translation with Introduction and Commentary*. AB 30. New York: Doubleday, 1982.

———. *The Gospel According to John I–XII: A New Translation with Introduction and Commentary*. AB 29. New York: Doubleday, 1966.

———. *An Introduction to the Gospel of John*. Edited by Francis J. Moloney. ABRL. New York: Doubleday, 2003.

Brown, Tricia Gates. *Spirit in the Writings of John: Pneumatology in Social-Scientific Perspective*. JSNTSupp 253. London: T. & T. Clark, 2003.

Büchsel, Friedrich. *Die Johannesbriefe*. Theologischer Handkommentar 17. Leipzig: Deichert, 1933.

———. "Zu den Johannesbriefen." *ZNW* 28 (1929) 235-241.

Bultmann, Rudolf. "Analyse des erten Johannesbriefes." In *Festgabe für Adolf Jülicher zum 70. Geburstag*, edited by Rudolf Bultmann and Hans Soden, 138–158. Tubingen: Mohr, 1927.

Bibliography

———. *The Gospel of John: A Commentary*. Translated by George Beasley-Murray, R. W. N. Hoare, and J. K Riches. Philadelphia: Fortress, 1971.

———. *The Johannine Epistles*. Hermeneia. Translated by R. Philip O'Hara with Lane C. McGaughy and Robert W. Funk. Philadelphia: Fortress, 1973.

———. "die kirchliche Redaktion des ersten Johannesbriefes." In *In Memorium Ernst Lohmeyer*, edited by W. Schmauch, 189–201. Stuttgart: Evangelisches, 1951.

———. *Theology of the New Testament*. 2 vols. Translated by Kendrick Grobel. New York: Scribner, 1951–1955.

Burge, Gary M. *The Anointed Community: The Holy Spirit in the Johannine Tradition*. Grand Rapids: Eerdmans, 1987.

Calley, Malcom J. C. *God's People*. Oxford: Oxford University Press, 1965.

Carson, D. A. *The Gospel according to John*. PNTC. Grand Rapids: Eerdmans, 1991.

Carter, Warren. *John and Empire: Initial Explorations*. New York: T. & T. Clark, 2008.

———. *John: Storyteller, Interpreter, Evangelist*. Peabody, MA: Hendrickson, 2006.

Carson, D. A. *The Gospel According to John*. PNTC. Grand Rapids: Eerdmans, 1991.

Charles, R. H. *A Critical and Exegetical Commentary on the Revelation to St. John*. 2 vols. ICC. Edinburgh: T. & T. Clark, 1920.

Charlesworth, James H. "The Gospel of John: Exclusivisim Caused by a Social Setting Different from That of Jesus (John 11:54 and 14:6)." In *Anti-Judaism in the Fourth Gospel*, edited by Reimund Bieringer, Didier Pollefeyt, and Frederique Vandecasteele-Vanneuville, 247–78. Louisville: Westminster John Knox, 2001.

———. *The Old Testament Pseudepigrapha Volume Two: Expansions of the "Old Testament" and Legends, Wisdom and Philosophical Literature, Prayers, Psalms, and Odes, Fragments of Lost Judeo-Hellenistic Works*. ABRL. New York: Doubleday, 1985.

Cicero. Translated by Harry Caplan et al. 29 vols. LCL. Cambridge, MA: Harvard University Press, 1954.

Cockerill, Gareth Lee. "Cerinthus." In *ABD*, edited by David Noel Freedman, 1:885. New York: Doubleday, 1992.

Csordas, Thomas J. *Language, Charisma, and Creativity: The Ritual Life of a Religious Movement*. Berkeley, CA: University of California Press, 1997.

Culpepper, R. Alan. *Anatomy of the Fourth Gospel*. Philadelphia: Fortress, 1983.

———. *The Gospel and Letters of John*. Interpreting Biblical Texts. Nashville: Abingdon, 1998.

———. "The Gospel of John as a Document of Faith in a Pluralistic Culture." In *What is John: Readers and Readings of the Fourth Gospel*, edited by Fernando F. Segovia, 107–27. Atlanta: Scholars, 1996.

———. *The Johannine School: An Evaluation of the Johannine-School Hypothesis Based on an Investigation of the Nature of Ancient Schools*. SBLDS 26. Missoula, MT: Scholars, 1975.

———. *John, the Son of Zebedee: The Life of a Legend*. SPNT. Columbia: University of South Carolina Press, 1994.

Culy, Martin M. *I, II, III John: A Handbook on the Greek Text*. Waco, TX: Baylor University, 2004.

Davies, W. D. "Reflections on Aspects of the Jewish Background of the Gospel of John." In *Exploring the Gospel of John: In Honor of D. Moody Smith*, edited by R. Alan Culpepper and C. Clifton Black, 43–64. Louisville: Westminster John Knox, 1996.

Dawson, Christopher. "What about Heretics: An Analysis of the Causes of Schism." *Commonweal* 36 (1942) 513–17.

Bibliography

Delling, Gerhard. "w[ra]" Translated by Geoffrey W. Bromiley. *TDNT*, edited by Gerhard Kittel, 9:675-81. Grand Rapids: Eerdmans, 1974.
Derrida, Jacques. *L'écriture et la difference*. Paris: Seuil, 1967.
Dobschütz, E., von. "Johanneische Studien, I." *ZNW* 8 (1907) 1-8.
Dodd, C. H. *The Johannine Epistles*. MNTC. New York: Harper & Row, 1946.
Doherty, Robert W. *The Hicksite Separation: A Sociological Analysis of Religious Schism in Early Nineteenth Century America*. New Brunswick, NJ: Rutgers University Press, 1967.
Douglas, Mary, ed. *Witchcraft Confessions and Accusations*. London: Tavistock, 1970.
Elliott, John H. *What Is Social-Scientific Criticism?* GBS. Minneapolis: Fortress, 1993.
Esler, Philip F. *Conflict and Identity in Romans: The Social Setting of Paul's Letter*. Minneapolis: Fortress, 2003.
Edwards, Ruth B. *The Johannine Epistles*. NTG. Sheffield: Sheffield Academic, 1996.
Fuglseth, Kåre Sigvald. *Johannine Sectarianism in Perspective: A Sociological, Historical, and comparative Analysis of Temple and Social Relationships in the Gospel of John, Philo, and Qumran*. NovTSup 119. Leiden: Brill, 2005.
Gamson, William. *The Strategy of Social Protest*. 2nd ed. Belmont, CA: Wadsworth, 1990.
García Martínez, Florentino. *The Dead Sea Scrolls Translated: The Qumran Texts in English*. 2nd edition. Translated by Wilfred G. E. Watson. Grand Rapids: Eerdmans, 1996.
García Martínez, Florentino, and Julio Trebolle Barrera. *The People of the Dead Sea Scrolls: Their Writings, Beliefs and Practices*. Translated by Wilfred G. E.   Watson.   Grand Rapids: Eerdmans, 1993.
Gaventa, Beverly Roberts. "The Archive of Excess: John 21 and the Problem of Narrative Closure." In *Exploring the Gospel of John: In Honor of D. Moody Smith*. Edited by R. Alan Culpepper and C. Clifton Black, 240-52. Louisville: Westminster John Knox, 1996.
Giudice, Marguerite, del. "Persia: Ancient Soul of Iran." *NG* 214, no. 2 (2008) 34-67.
Gore, Charles. *The Epistles of St. John*. London: Murray, 1920.
Grayston, Kenneth. *The Johannine Epistles: Based on the Revised Standard Version*. NCB. Grand Rapids: Eerdmans, 1984.
Greenslade, S. L. *Schism in the Early Church*. London: SCM, 1953.
Hakola, Raimo. *Identity Matters: John, the Jews and Jewishness*. NovTSup 118. Leiden: Brill, 2005.
Harding, Susan F. "Convicted by the Holy Spirit: The Rhetoric of Fundamental Baptist Conversion." In *Across the Boundaries of Belief: Contemporary Issues in the Anthropology of Religion*, edited by Morton Klass and Maxine K. Weisgrau, 381-401. Boulder, CO: Westview, 1999.
Harnack, Adolf. "Über den dritten Johannesbrief." *TU* 15, no. 3 (1897) 3-27.
Harner, Philip B. *What Are They Saying About the Catholic Epistles?* New York: Paulist, 2004.
Harrington, Wilfrid J. *Revelation*. Sacra Pagina 16. Collegeville, MN: Liturgical, 1993.
Heath, Malcolm. "Invention." In *Handbook of Classical Rhetoric in the Hellenistic Period: 330B.C. to A.D. 400*, edited by Stanley Porter, 89-119. Leiden: Brill, 1997.
Heger, Paul. *Cult as the Catalyst for Division: Cult Disputes as the Motive for Schism in the Pre-70 Pluralistic Environment*. Leiden: Brill, 2007.
———. *The Three Biblical Altar Laws*. BZAW 279. Berlin: de Gruyter, 1999.
Hemer, Colin J. *The Letters to the Seven Churches of Asia in Their Local Setting*. BRS. Grand Rapids: Eerdmans, 1989.

BIBLIOGRAPHY

Hengel, Martin. *The Johannine Question*. Translated by John Bowden. Philadelphia: Trinity, 1989.

Hill, Charles E. "Cerinthus, Gnostic of Chiliast? A New Solution to an Old Problem." *JECS* 8 (2000) 135–172.

Hillis, Brian V. *Can Two Walk Together Unless They Be Agreed? American Religious Schisms in the 1970s*. New York: Carlson, 1991.

Houlden, J. L. *The Johannine Epistles*. HNTC. New York: Harper and Row, 1973.

———. *The Johannine Epistles*. 2nd rev. ed. BNTC. London: Continuum, 2001.

Hurtado, Larry W. *Lord Jesus Christ: Devotion to Jesus in Earliest Christianity*. Grand Rapids: Eerdmans, 2003.

Johnson, Allan G. *The Blackwell Dictionary of Sociology: A User's Guide to Sociological Language*. Cambridge, MA: Blackwell Reference, 1995.

Johnson, Benton. "On Founders and Followers: Some Factors in the Development of New Religious Movements." In *Across the Boundaries of Belief: Contemporary Issues in the Anthropology of Religion*, edited by Morton Klass and Maxine K. Weisgrau, 367–80. Boulder, CO: Westview, 1999.

Johnson, Brian D. "'Salvation Is from the Jews': Judaism in the Gospel of John." In *New Currents through John: A Global Perspective*, edited by Francisco Lozada Jr. and Tom Thatcher, 83–99. RBS 54. Atlanta: Scholars, 2006.

Johnson, Luke T. "The New Testament's Anti-Jewish Slander and the Conventions of Ancient Polemic." *JBL* 108, no. 3 (1989) 419–41.

Johnson, Thomas F. *1, 2, and 3 John*. NIBCNT 17. Peabody, MA: Hendrickson, 1993.

Johnston, George. *The Spirit Paraclete in the Gospel of John*. New Testament Studies Monograph 12. Cambridge: Cambridge University Press, 1970.

de Jonge, M. *De Brieven van Johannes*. De Prediking van het Nieuwe Testament: Nijkerk, 1973.

———. "The Gospel and the Epistles of John Read against the Background of the History of the Johannine Communities." In *What We Have Heard from the Beginning: The Past, Present, and Future of Johannine Studies*, edited by Tom Thatcher, 127–44. Waco, TX: Baylor University Press, 2007.

Josephus. Translated by H. St. J. Thackerya et al. 13 vols. LCL. Cambridge, MA: Harvard University Press, 1997–2004.

Kahlos, Maijastina. *Debate and Dialogue: Christian and Pagan Cultures c. 360–430*. Ashgate New Critical Thinking in Religion, Theology and Biblical Studies. Hampshire, UK: Ashgate, 2007.

Käsemann, Ernst. "Ketzer und Zeuge: Zum johanneischen Verfasserproblem." *ZTK* 48 (1951) 292–311.

Katz, Steven T. "Issues in the Separation of Judaism and Christianity after 70 C.E.: A Reconsideration." *JBL* 103 (1984) 43–76.

Keener, Craig. *The Gospel of John: A Commentary*. 2 vols. Peabody, MA: Hendrickson, 2003.

Kennedy, George A. "The Genres of Rhetoric." In *Handbook of Classical Rhetoric in the Hellenistic Period (330 B.C.–A.D. 400)*, edited by Stanley E. Porter, 43–50. Leiden: Brill 1997.

Kierspel, Lars. *The Jews and the World in the Fourth Gospel: Parallelism, Function, and Context*. WUNT 2/220. Tübingen: Mohr/Siebeck, 2006.

Kimmelman, Reuven. "*Birkat Haminim* and the Lack of Evidence for an A Christian Jewish Prayer in Late Antiquity." In *Jewish and Christian Self-Definition*, edited by

Bibliography

E. P. Sanders with A. I. Baumgarten and Alan Mendelson, 391–403. Philadelphia: Fortress, 1981.

Klauck, Hans-Josef. *Der Erste Johannesbrief.* Evangelisch-Katholischer Kommentar zum Neuen Testament 23/1. Zurich: Benziger, 1991.

———. *Der Zweite und Dritte Johannesbrief.* Evangelisch-Katholischer Kommentar zum Neuen Testament 23/2. Zurich: Benziger, 1992.

———. "Internal Opponents: the Treatment of the Secessionists in the First Epistle of John." Translated by Robert Nowell. In *Truth and its Victims: Concilium* 200, edited by Willem Beuken, Sean Freyne, and Anton Weiler: 55–65. Edinburgh: T. & T. Clark, 1988.

———. "Zur rhetorischen Analyse der Johannesbriefe. *ZNW* 1 (1990) 205–224.

Klijn, A. F. J., and G. J. Reinink. *Patristic Evidence for Jewish-Christian Sects.* NovTSup 36. Leiden, Brill, 1973.

Koester, Craig. *Symbolism in the Fourth Gospel: Meaning, Mystery, Community.* Rev. ed. Minneapolis: Fortress, 2003.

Koester, Helmut. *History and Literature of Early Christianity: Introduction to the New Testament.* Vol. 2. 2nd ed. New York: de Gruyter, 2000.

Kossen, H. B. "Who Were the Greeks of John XII.20?" In *Studies in John: Presented to Dr. J. N. Sevenster on the Occasion of His Seventieth Birthday,* edited by W. C. van Unnik et al., 97–110. NovTSup 24. Leiden: Brill, 1970.

Köstenberger, Andreas J. *John.* BECNT on the New Testament. Grand Rapids: Baker Academic, 2004.

Kruse, Colin G. *The Letters of John.* PNTC. Grand Rapids: Eerdmans, 2000.

Kümmel, Werner Georg. *Introduction to the New Testament.* Translated by Howard Clark Kee. Rev. Eng. ed. Nashville: Abingdon, 1975.

Lambrecht, Jan. "'Synagogues of Satan' (Rev. 2:9 and 3:9): Anti-Judaism in the Book of Revelation." In *Anti-Judaism in the Fourth Gospel,* edited by Reimund Bieringer, Didier Pollefeyt, and Frederique Vandecasteele-Vanneuville; 279–92. Louisville: Westminster John Knox, 2001.

Langbrandtner, Wolfgang. *Weltferner Gott oder Gott der Liebe: Die Ketzerstreit in der johanneischen Kirche.* BBET 6. Frankfurt: Lang, 1977.

Law, Robert. *The Tests of Life: A Study of the First Epistle of St. John.* 3rd ed. Edinburgh: T. & T. Clark, 1914.

Leatham, Miguel C. "'Shaking Out the Mat': Schism and Organizational Transformation at a Mexican Ark of the Virgin." *JSSR* 42, no. 2 (2003) 175–87.

Lewis, James R. "American Indian Prophets." In *When Prophets Die: The Postcharismatic Fate of New Religious Movements,* edited by Timothy Miller, 47–57. New York: State University of New York Press, 1991.

Liebman, R. C., J. R. Sutton, and R. Wuthnow. "Exploring the Social Sources of Denominationalism: Schism in American Protestant Denominations, 1890–1980." *ASR* 53 (1988) 343–52.

Lieu, Judith. *I, II, & III John: A Commentary.* The New Testament Library. Louisville: Westminster John Knox, 2008.

———. *The Second and Third Epistles of John.* Studies of the New Testament and Its World. Edinburgh: T. & T. Clark, 1986.

———. *The Theology of the Johannine Epistles.* New Testament Theology. Cambridge: Cambridge University Press, 1991.

Bibliography

Lim, Timothy H. *The Dead Sea Scrolls: A Very Short Introduction*. Oxford: Oxford University Press, 2005.
Lincoln, Andrew T. *The Gospel according to Saint John*. BNTC. Peabody, MA: Hendrickson, 2005.
Lindars, Barnabas. *The Gospel of John*. NCB. London: Oliphants, 1972.
Lindars, Barnabas, Ruth B. Edwards, and John M. Court. *The Johannine Literature*. Sheffield: Sheffield Academic, 2000.
Lorein, G. W. *The Antichrist Theme in the Intertestamental Period*. JSPSup 44. London: T. & T. Clark, 2003.
Mack, Burton L. *Rhetoric and the New Testament*. GBS, New Testament Series. Minneapolis: Fortress, 1989.
Malatesta, Edward. *Interiority and Covenant*. AnBib 69. Rome: Biblical Institute, 1978.
Malhberbe, Abraham J. "The Inhospitality of Diotrephes." In *God's Christ and his People: Studies in Honour of Nils Alstrup Dahl*, edited by Jacob Jervell and Wayne A. Meeks, 222–32. Oslo: Universitetsforlaget, 1977.
———. *The Letters to the Thessalonians: A New Translation with Introduction and Commentary*. AB 32B. New York: Doubleday, 2000.
Malina, Bruce J. *The New Testament World: Insights from Cultural Anthropology*. 3rd ed. Louisville: Westminster John Knox, 2001.
Malina, Bruce J., and Jerome H. Neyrey. *Calling Jesus Names: The Social Value of Labels in Matthew*. FF. Sonoma, CA: Polebridge, 1988.
Malina, Bruce J., and John J. Pilch. *Social-Science Commentary on the Book of Revelation*. Minneapolis: Fortress, 2000.
Malina, Bruce J., and Richard L. Rohrbaugh. *Social Science Commentary on the Gospel of John*. Minneapolis: Augsburg Fortress, 1998.
Marshall, I. Howard. *The Epistles of John*. NICNT. Grand Rapids: Eerdmans, 1978.
Martyn, J. Louis. "A Gentile Mission That Replaced an Earlier Jewish Mission?" In *Exploring the Gospel of John: In Honor of D. Moody Smith*, edited by R. Alan Culpepper and C. Clifton Black, 124–44. Louisville: Westminster John Knox, 1996.
———. *History and Theology in the Fourth Gospel*. 3rd ed. NTL. Louisville: Westminster John Knox, 2003.
———. "The Johannine Community among Jewish and Other Early Christian Communities." In *What We Have Heard from the Beginning: The Past, Present, and Future of Johannine Studies*, edited by Tom Thatcher, 183–90. Waco, TX: Baylor University Press, 2007.
Meeks, Wayne A. "The Man from Heaven in Johannine Sectarianism." *JBL* 91 (1972) 44–72.
———. *The Prophet-King: Moses Traditions and the Johannine Christology*. NovTSup 14. Leiden: Brill, 1967.
Meier, John P. *A Marginal Jew: Rethinking the Historical Jesus*. 3 vols. ABRL. New York: Doubleday, 1991–2001.
Melton, J. Gordon. "Introduction: When Prophets Die: The Succession Crisis in New Religions." In *When Prophets Die: The Postcharismatic Fate of New Religious Movements*, edited by Timothy Miller, 1–12. New York: State University of New York Press, 1991.
Miller, Norman. "Formal Organization and Schismogenesis." Unpublished paper. Chicago, 1963.

Bibliography

Moberly, R. W. L. "'Test the Spirits': God, Love, and Critical Discernment in 1 John 4." In *The Holy Spirit and Christian Origins: Essays in Honor of James D. G. Dunn*, edited by Graham N. Stanton et al., 296–307. Grand Rapids: Eerdmans, 2006.

Moloney, Francis J. *Glory Not Dishonor: Reading John 13–21*. Minneapolis: Fortress, 1998.

———. *The Gospel of John*. SP 4. Collegeville: Liturgical, 1998.

Mooney, Annabelle. *The Rhetoric of Religious "Cults": Terms of Use and Abuse*. New York: Palgrave MacMillan, 2005.

Morris, Leon. *The Gospel according to John*. Rev. ed. NICNT. Grand Rapids: Eerdmans, 1995.

Mounce, Robert H. *The Book of Revelation*. NICNT. Grand Rapids: Eerdmans, 1977.

Murdock, George P. *Theories of Illness: A World Survey*. Pittsburgh: University of Pittsburgh Press, 1980.

Murphy-O'Connor, Jerome. "Teacher of Righteousness." In *ABD*, edited by David Noel Freedman, 6:340–41. New York: Doubleday, 1992.

Myllykoski, Matti. "Cerinthus." In *A Companion to Second-Century Christian "Heretics,"* edited by Antti Marjanen and Patri Luomanen, 213–46. VCSup 76. Leiden: Brill, 2005.

Nauck, Wolfgang. *Die Tradition und der Charakter des ersten Johannesbriefes*. WUNT 4. Tubingen: Mohr, 1957.

Nelson, Geoffrey K. *Cults, New Religions & Religious Creativity*. London: Routledge, 1987.

Neufeld, Detmar. *Reconceiving Texts as Speech Acts: An Analysis of 1 John*. Leiden: Brill, 1994.

Neyrey, Jerome H, SJ. *The Gospel of John*. NCBC. New York: Cambridge University, 2007.

———. *An Ideology of Revolt: John's Christology in Social-Science Perspective*. Philadelphia: Fortress, 1988.

Niebuhr, H. Richard. *The Social Sources of Denominationalism*. New York: Holt, 1929.

Nyomarkay, Joseph. *Charisma and Factionalism in the Nazi Party*. Minneapolis: University of Minnesota Press, 1967.

O'Neill, J. C. *The Puzzle of 1 John: A New Examination of Origins*. London: SPCK, 1966.

Osborne, Grant R. *Revelation*. BECNT. Grand Rapids: Baker, 2002.

Painter, John. *1, 2, and 3 John*. SP 18. Collegeville: Liturgical, 2002.

———. *John: Witness and Theologian*. London: SPCK, 1975.

———. "The 'Opponents' in 1 John." *NTS* 32 (1986) 48–71.

———. *The Quest for the Messiah: The History, Literature and Theoloy of the Johannine Community*. Edinburgh: T. & T. Clark, 1991.

Pancaro, Severino. *The Law in the Fourth Gospel: The Torah and the Gospel, Moses and Jesus, Judaism and Christianity according to John*. NovTSup 42. Leiden: Brill, 1975.

Parker, Doug, and Helen Parker. *The Secret Sect*. Pendle Hill, Australia: privately published, 1982.

Perelman, C., and L. Olbrechts-Tyteca, *The New Rhetoric: A Treatise on Argumentation*. Translated by J. Wilkinson and P. Weaver. Notre Dame: University of Notre Dame, 1969.

Perkins, Pheme. *The Johannine Epistles*. New Testament Message 21. Wilmington, DE: Glazier, 1979.

Plummer, Alfred. *The Epistles of S. John: With Notes, Introduction and Appendices*. Cambridge Greek Testament for Schools and Colleges. Cambridge: Cambridge University Press, 1938.

Pope, Liston. *Millhands and Preachers*. New Haven: Yale University Press, 1942.

Bibliography

Poythress, V. S. "Johannine Authorship and the Use of Intersentence Conjunctions in the Book of Revelation." *WTJ* 47 (1985) 329–36.

Price, S. R. F. *Rituals and Power: The Roman Imperial Cult in Asia Minor.* Cambridge: Cambridge University Press, 1984.

Puech, Émile. "The Essenes and Qumran, the Teacher and the Wicked Priest, the Origins." In *Enoch and Qumran Origins: New Light on a Forgotten Connection,* edited by Gabriele Boccaccini, 298–301. Grand Rapids: Eerdmans, 2005.

Quintilian. Translated by H. E. Butler. 4 vols. LCL. Cambridge, MA: Harvard University Press, 1921–1958.

Reed, David. "Rethinking John's Social Setting: Hidden Transcript, Anti-Language, and the Negotiation of the Empire." *BTB* 36, no. 3 (2006) 93–106.

Reinhartz, Adele. *Befriending the Beloved Disciple: A Jewish Reading of the Gospel of John.* New York: Continuum, 2005.

———. "The Johannine Community and Its Jewish Neighbors: A Reappraisal." In *"What is John?,"* edited by Fernando F. Segovia, 2:111–38. SBLSymS 7. Atlanta: Scholars, 1998.

———. "Response: Reading History in the Fourth Gospel." In *What We Have Heard from the Beginning: The Past, Present, and Future of Johannine Studies,* edited by Tom Thatcher, 191–94. Waco, TX: Baylor University Press, 2007.

Rensberger, David. *1 John, 2 John, 3 John.* ANTC. Nashville: Abingdon, 1997.

Ridderbos, Herman. *The Gospel of John: A Theological Commentary.* Translated by John Vriend. Grand Rapids: Eerdmans, 1997.

Robbins, Vernon K. *Exploring the Texture of Texts: A Guide to Socio-Rhetorical Interpretation.* Harrisburg, PA: Trinity, 1996.

———. *The Tapestry of Early Christian Discourse: Rhetoric, Society, and Ideology.* London: Routledge, 1996.

Roberts, Alexander and James Donaldson, editors. *The Ante-Nicene Fathers.* 10 vols. Grand Rapids: Eerdmans, 1993.

Robinson, John A. T. *Twelve New Testament Studies.* London: SCM, 1962.

Rochford, E. Burke. "Factionalism, Group Defection, and Schism in the Hare Krishna Movement." *JSSR* 28 (1989) 162–79.

Roloff, Jürgen. *The Revelation of John: A Continental Commentary.* Translated by John E. Alsup. CC. Minneapolis: Fortress, 1993.

Saliba, John A. *Understanding New Religious Movements.* 2nd ed. Walnut Creek, CA: AltaMira, 2003.

Schnackenburg, Rudolf. *The Gospel according to Saint John.* 3 vols. Translated by Kevin Smyth et al. New York: Crossroad, 1987.

———. *The Johannine Epistles: Introduction and Commentary.* Translated by Reginald and Ilse Fuller. New York: Crossroad, 1992.

Schneemelcher, Wilhelm, ed. *New Testament Apocrypha.* 2 vols. Translated and edited by R. McL. Wilson. Rev. ed. Louisville: Westminster John Knox, 1989.

Schnelle, Udo. *Antidocetic Christology in the Gospel of John.* Translated by Linda M. Maloney. Minneapolis: Fortress, 1992.

———. *Das Evangelium nach Johannes.* THKNT. Leipzig: Evangelische, 2000.

———. *The History and Theology of the New Testament Writings.* Translated by M. Eugene Boring. Minneapolis: Fortress, 1998.

Scobie, Charles H. H. "Johannine Geography." *Studies in Religion* 11, no. 1 (1982) 77–84.

Bibliography

Schoedel, William R. *Ignatius of Antioch: A Commentary on the Letters of Ignatius.* Hermeneia. Minneapolis: Augsburg Fortress, 1985.

Schoeps, Hans Joachim. *Jewish Christianity: Factional Disputes in the Early Church.* Translated by Douglas R. A. Hare. Philadelphia: Fortress, 1969.

Schüssler Fiorenza, Elizabeth. "The Quest for the Johannine School: The Apocalypse and the Fourth Gospel." *NTS* 23 (1977) 402–27.

Sloyan, Gerard. *John.* IBC. Louisville: Westminster John Knox, 1988.

Smalley, Stephen S. *1, 2, 3 John.* WBC 51. Nashville: Nelson, 1984.

———. *1, 2, 3 John.* Rev. ed. WBC 51. Nashville: Nelson, 2007.

———. *John: Evangelist & Interpreter.* 2nd ed. New Testament Profiles. Downer's Grove, IL: InterVarsity, 1998.

———. *The Revelation to John: A Commentary on the Greek Text of the Apocalypse.* Downer's Grove, IL: InterVarsity, 2005.

———. *Thunder and Love: John's Revelation and John's Community.* Milton Keynes, UK: Word, 1994.

Smith, D. Moody. *The Composition and Order of the Fourth Gospel: Bultmann's Literary Theory.* YPR 10. New Haven: Yale University Press, 1965

———. *First, Second, and Third John.* IBC. Louisville: John Knox, 1991.

———. *Johannine Christianity: Essays on its Setting, Sources and Theology.* Edinburgh: T. & T. Clark, 1999.

Stamps, Dennis L. "The Johannine Writings." In *Handbook of Classical Rhetoric in the Hellenistic Period (330 B.C.–A.D. 400)*, edited by Stanley E. Porter, 609–32. Leiden: Brill 1997.

Stark, Rodney. *The Rise of Christianity: How the Obscure, Marginal Jesus Movement Became the Dominant Religious Force n the Western World in a Few Centuries.* San Francisco: HarperSanFrancisco, 1997.

Stark, Rodney, and William Sims Bainbridge. *The Future of Religion: Secularization, Revival and Cult Formation.* Berkeley: University of California Press, 1985.

Staub, Jacob J. "Reconstructionist Judaism." In *The Encyclopedia of Judaism*, edited by Jacob Neusner, Alan J. Avery-Peck, and William Scott Green, 4:2247–60. 2nd ed. Leiden: Brill, 2005.

Stone, Michael Edward. *Fourth Erza: A Commentary on the Book of Fourth Ezra.* Edited by Frank Moore Cross. Hermeneia. Minneapolis: Fortress, 1990.

Stott, John R. W. *The Letters of John.* TNTC 19. Downer's Grove, IL: InterVarsity, 1988.

Strecker, Georg. "Chiliasm and Docetism in the Johannine School." *ABR* 38 (199) 45–61.

———. *The Johannine Letters.* Translated by Linda M. Maloney. Hermeneia. Minneapolis: Fortress, 1996.

Stromberg, Peter G. *Language and Self-Transformation: A Study of the Christian Conversion Narrative.* Cambridge: Cambridge University Press, 1993.

Sugit, J. N. "I John 5:21: TEKNIA, FULACATE EAUTA APO TWN EIDWLWN." *JTS* 36 (1985) 386–90.

Swete, Henry Barclay. *The Apocalypse of St. John: The Greek Text with Introduction, Notes, and Indices.* 1907. Reprint, Grand Rapids: Eerdmans, 1951.

Talbert, Charles H. *Reading John: A Literary and Theological Commentary on the Fourth Gospel and the Johannine Epistles.* New York: Crossroad, 1992.

Tenney, Merrill C. *John: The Gospel of Belief: An Analytic Study of the Text.* Grand Rapids: Eerdmans, 1976.

Bibliography

Thatcher, Tom. "The New Current through John: The Old 'New Look' and the New Critical Orthodoxy." In *New Currents Through John: A Global Perspective,* edited by Francisco Lozada Jr. and Tom Thatcher, 1–26. RBS 54. Atlanta: Scholars, 2006.

Thomas, John Christopher. *The Pentecostal Commentary on 1 John, 2 John, 3 John.* Pentecostal Commentary, New Testament. Cleveland: Pilgrim, 2004.

Thompson, Marianne Meye. *1-3 John.* IVP New Testament Commentary. Downers Grove, IL: InterVarsity, 1992.

Trible, Phyllis. *Rhetorical Criticism: Context, Method, and the Book of Jonah.* GBS, Old Testament. Minneapolis: Fortress, 1994.

Tubeville, Gus. "Religious Schism in the Methodist Church: A Sociological Analysis of the Pine Grove Case." *Rural Sociology* 14 (1949) 29–39.

Turner, Victor. *Dramas, Fields, and Metaphors: Symbolic Action in Human Society.* Ithaca, NY: Cornell University Press, 1975.

Van der Horst, Pieter. "The *Birkat Ha-Minim* in Recent Research." *ExpTim* 105 (1994) 363–68.

Vermes, Geza. *The Complete Dead Sea Scrolls in English.* New York: Penguin, 1997.

———. *An Introduction to the Complete Dead Sea Scrolls.* Minneapolis: Fortress, 1999.

Vogler, Werner. *Die Briefe des Johannes.* THKNT 17. Leipzig: Evangelische, 1993.

Vouga, François. "La reception de la théologie johannique dans les epîtres." In *La Communauté Johannique et son Histoire: La trajectoire de l'évangelile de Jean aux deux premiers siècles,* edited by Jean-Daniel Kaestli, Jean-Michel Poffet, and Jean Zumstein, 283–302. Geneva: Labor et Fides, 1990.

Waetjen, Herman C. *The Gospel of the Beloved Disciple: A Work in Two Editions.* New York: T. & T. Clark, 2005.

Wallis, Roy, ed. *Sectarianism: Analyses of Religious and Non-Religious Sects.* New York: Wiley, 1975.

Wallis, Roy. *The Elementary Forms of New Religious Life.* London: Routledge, 1984.

———. *Salvation and Protest: Studies of Social and Religious Movements.* New York: St. Martin's, 1979.

Watson, Duane F. "1 John 2:12–14 as *Distributio, Conduplicatio,* and *Expolitio*: A Rhetorical Understanding." *JSNT* 35 (1989) 97–110.

———. "Amplification Techniques in 1 John: The Interaction of Rhetorical Style and Invention." *JSNT* 51 (1993) 99–123.

———. "An Epideictic Strategy for Increasing Adherence to Community Values: 1 John 1:1—2:27." *Proceedings of the Eastern Great Lakes and Midwest Biblical Societies* 11 (1991) 144–52.

———. "A Rhetorical Analysis of 2 John according to Greco-Roman Convention." *NTS* 35 (1989) 104–30.

———. "A Rhetorical Analysis of 3 John: A Study in Epistolary Rhetoric." *CBQ* 51 (1989) 479–501.

Weber, Max. *The Theory of Social and Economic Organization.* Edited by Talcott Parsons. Translated by A. M. Henderson and Talcott Parsons. Glencoe, IL: Free, 1947.

Wengst, Klaus. *Häresie und Orthodoxie im Spiegel des ersten Johannesbriefes.* OTKNT 16. Würzburg: Gütersloh, 1976.

Westcott, Brooke Foss. *The Epistles of St. John.* London: MacMillan, 1883.

———. *The Gospel according to St. John.* 2 vol. London: Hazell, Watson and Viney, 1908.

Whale, P. "The Lamb of John: Some Myths about the Vocabulary of the Johannine Literature." *JBL* 106 (1987) 289–95.

Bibliography

Whitacre, Rodney A. *Johannine Polemic: The Role of Tradition and Theology.* SBLDS 67. Chico, CA: 1982.

Wilson, Bryan R. *The Noble Savages: The Primitive Origins of Charisma and Its Contemporary Survival.* Berkeley: University of California Press, 1975.

———. *Sects and Society: A Sociological Study of the Elim Tabernacle, Christian Science, and Christadelphians.* Berkeley: University of California Press: 1961.

———. *The Social Dimensions of Sectarianism: Sects and New Religious Movements in Contemporary Society.* Oxford: Clarendon, 1990.

Wilson, John. "The Sociology of Schism." In *A Sociological Yearbook of Religion in Britain,* edited by Michael Hill, 4:1–20. London: SCM, 1971.

Witherington, Ben, III. *John's Wisdom: A Commentary on the Fourth Gospel.* Louisville: Westminster John Knox, 1995.

———. *Letters and Homilies for Hellenized Christians.* Volume 1, *A Socio-Rhetorical Commentary on Titus, 1–2 Timothy and 1–3 John.* Downers Grove, IL: IVP Academic, 2006.

———. *Revelation.* NCBC. Cambridge: Cambridge University Press, 2003.

Wurm, Alois. *Die Irrlehrer im ItenJohannes Brief.* Freiburg: Herder, 1903.

Yarbrough, Robert W. *1–3 John.* BECNT. Grand Rapids: Baker, 2008.

Yinger, J. Milton. *Religion, Society, and the Individual.* New York: Macmillan, 1957.

Zald, Mayer, and Roberta Ash. "Social Movement Organizations: Growth, Decay, and Change." *Social Forces* 44 (1966) 327–41.

Zuckerman, Phil. *Strife in the Sanctuary: Religious Schism in a Jewish Community.* Walnut Creek, CA: Altamira, 1999.

www.ingramcontent.com/pod-product-compliance
Lightning Source LLC
Chambersburg PA
CBHW051940160426
43198CB00013B/2233